ENGAGING
THE STORY OF GOD

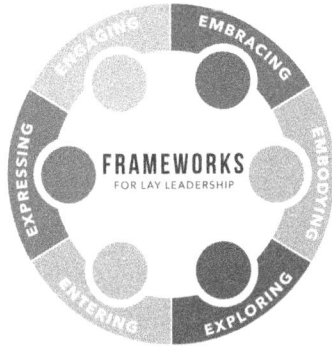

FRAMEWORKS
FOR LAY LEADERSHIP

Rob A. Fringer, series editor

ENGAGING
THE STORY OF GOD

Rob A. Fringer

Global Nazarene Publications

ISBN 978-1-56344-891-1
rev20180828

Global Nazarene Publication
Lenexa, Kansas (USA)

Copyright © 2018
Rob A. Fringer

DIGITAL PRINTING

TABLE OF CONTENTS

FRAMEWORKS
FOR LAY LEADERSHIP

Scripture tells us that believers are "a royal priesthood" (1 Peter 2:9). This means that all Christians, in one form or another, are called into places of ministry and leadership. Not only is this a great privilege, it is also a great responsibility. Men and women desiring to serve in church leadership in some capacity undergo basic training to assure that they understand the foundations of the Christian faith and of our Nazarene identity. This includes a deepening knowledge and appreciation of Scripture, Theology, Ministry, Mission, History, and Holiness. *Frameworks for Lay Leadership* is a series of six books designed to do just that—equip lay leaders for ministry in the Church, whether local, district, or general. These books have the greatest impact when they are read, processed, applied, and contextualised in partnership with a qualified mentor.

Welcome to this journey of transformation!

ENGAGING THE STORY OF GOD
EXPLORING A WESLEYAN THEOLOGY
EMBODYING A THEOLOGY OF MINISTRY AND LEADERSHIP
ENTERING THE MISSION OF GOD
EXPRESSING A NAZARENE IDENTITY
EMBRACING A DOCTRINE OF HOLINESS

FOREWORD

Frameworks for Lay Leadership is a series of six books designed to equip laypeople in the Wesleyan-holiness tradition for ministry and leadership in a local church. The Church of the Nazarene defines a "church" as:

> *Any group*
> *that meets regularly for spiritual nurture, worship, or instruction*
> *at an announced time and place,*
> *with an identified leader,*
> *and aligned with the mission and message*
> *of the Church of the Nazarene*
> *can be recognized as a church*
> *and reported as such for district and general church statistics.*
> (Nazarene Essentials)

This definition is grounded in biblical theology as well as the practice of the Early Church. Being a church should not be confined to a particular kind of building, or any building at all. Churches can meet at any time and at any place. In our context of the 21st Century, this definition of "church" should encourage and release laypeople to live out their own callings and gifts. That is to say, church leadership is not restricted to ordained clergy. From the beginning, God has used both women and men, young and old, educated and uneducated, rich and poor to carry out his mission in the world.

The Manual of the Church of the Nazarene (paragraphs 503-503.9) makes provision for qualified lay ministers, both male and female, to serve in ministerial leadership under the supervision of a pastor and church board or a district superintendent and district advisory board. However, before this can take place, lay ministers must clearly understand who we are, what we believe, and some of the practices that guide public ministry.

Nazarenes from the beginning have been known for theological tolerance. Two maxims capture this spirit, "In essentials, unity; in non-essentials, liberty; and in all things, charity" and "If your heart is as my heart, give me your hand." It is important, then, that lay ministers understand our core beliefs and distinctions (non-negotiables such as our theological understanding of God and scripture, our Wesleyan-holiness emphasis, and our ordination of women) as well as those areas where we may embrace various interpretations and opinions (such as the form of baptism, our understanding of how God created the universe, divine healing, the nature and timing of the Second Coming of Christ, and church structures).

Frameworks for Lay Leadership is designed to guide laypeople through a validated course of study in order to lead a variety of ministries in the Church of the Nazarene. This is particularly helpful in contexts where there are no ordained clergy to plant or lead new congregations or oversee existing ones. Upon completion of this course of study, under the guidance of an ordained Nazarene minister, a certificate of lay ministry may be issued by a local church board or a district advisory board.

John Moore
Regional Education/Clergy Development, Asia Pacific Region
Field Strategy Coordinator, Australia/New Zealand

CHAPTER 1

INTRODUCING THE STORY OF GOD

The Bible is the most popular book in history. It was the first book produced on a printing press, and more copies have been translated and printed than any other book in the world. However, for Christians, it is more than a book; it is the Word of God. While most Christians would see this as an entirely positive claim, this truth is more complex than we often acknowledge, and there are negative connotations possible if such a claim is not properly examined and understood. Several questions come to mind: What does "Word of God" mean? Would all Christians be able to agree on the same definition? Is the Bible authoritative? If so, from where does the authority come? How is the Bible inspired? Is it possible to revere the Bible too much? Because Scripture is so important, we must do the hard work of examining what we believe about this book and why. Christians should not be afraid to probe their own beliefs in order to understand them at a deeper level and refine them as needed. This type of critical (i.e., careful or analytical) examination strengthens our faith and enables us to speak with greater assurance and credibility.

Besides studying and acknowledging what we believe about the place of Scripture, it is also important that we understand how to read and interpret Scripture. The Bible is made up of sixty-six separate books each with its own particular historical data, literary structure, and purpose. Furthermore, these various books were selected, confirmed, ordered, and interpreted by the Church universal, and as such, they have significant theological importance individually and as a whole. When we read Scripture, we are part of something much larger than ourselves, and this should give us pause. We want to honour both the individual books as well as the larger theological narrative of the Bible in our interpretations. This requires us to take biblical interpretation seriously and for us to be attuned to the Spirit's voice at work in the body of Christ through this process. In order to do this effectively, we must be aware of various ways of engaging Scripture at a deeper level, and of looking at it from different angles.

Our own theological framework (or tradition) becomes an important factor in the study of Scripture, and we must also be aware of the potential pitfalls of such a framework if grasped too tightly or if used as the sole interpretive lens. Nevertheless, we must also recognise that our own theological framework is important and has shaped our understanding of God and God's activity in the world. It formed our understanding of the place of Scripture and of how we interpret it. The Scriptures are the basis for our theology, but our theology often controls our interpretation of any given passage of the Bible. Instead of hiding from this seeming dilemma, we must embrace them both; Scripture and theology must acknowledge each other's role. Furthermore, we will see how reason and experience also play a part in how we interpret the Bible.

The purpose of this book is to guide us into a deeper understanding of Scripture, its grand narrative, and its interpretation. Multiple challenging and technical concepts will be introduced along the way that may stretch our thinking. This should be seen as a positive thing. It is part of a process of maturing in our Christian faith and growing deeper in our knowledge and love of God.

QUESTIONS FOR REFLECTION

1. What do you mean when you say the Bible is the Word of God?

2. What do you see as the positive and negative connotations of allowing your theological background to shape the way you read and understand Scripture?

CHAPTER 2

UNDERSTANDING THE STORY OF GOD

There are many substantial and weighty terms used to speak about the Bible. We speak about its *authority*, its *inspiration*, and about its *inerrant* or *infallible* nature. None of these terms have a single definition; it is truer to speak about a spectrum of meanings. In this section, we will explore these terms in more depth. The point of this endeavour is not to establish a single, concrete definition. Rather, we want to understand the complexity of such language, especially as it pertains to something as sacred as the Word of God. This beginning exercise is significant as it will help set the stage for the dynamic pursuit of discovering meaning in the Scriptures.

When discussing meaning, we must remember the role of context in its establishment; words have meaning in context,[1] and contexts are not limited to paragraphs on a page. It matters who said it, when they said it, why they said it, to whom they said it, the culture in which they said it, and even the experiences they had that shaped how they said it. This is not to say that the discovery of meaning is unattainable or that all meaning is subjective, changing from person to person. Instead, it is a reminder of how relationally-grounded meaning is. This is because we are relational beings created by a relational God. When we lose sight of this truth and try to turn everything into objective formulas, we miss out on the dynamic exploration and growth of relationship.

The Authority of Scripture

The word *authority* can have positive and negative connotations. We recognise how complex the concept of authority is when we think of various world leaders. Some of these men and women use their authority to control and manipulate in order to gain greater power, money, and prestige for themselves. Others use their authority to fight for freedom, justice, and equality and to give others the power to make their own decisions.

Christians tend to accept the authority of the Bible without much hesitation. Most would readily agree that the Bible is authoritative based on their belief that it is the Word of God. Still, the question must be asked, "What do we mean when we say the Bible is authoritative?" Our answer to this question has implications for how we live and how we treat others. If we are not careful, Scripture easily becomes a tool used to control people and situations,[2] and any authority it may have is ultimately lost.

It is important for us to distinguish between *Scripture as authority* and *Scripture as revealing authority*. This difference appears slight, but it has huge implications, often without us realising it. *Scripture as authority* sees the Bible as a lifeless book, kind of like a dictionary or encyclopaedia, where we go to get information; it makes Scripture an end in itself. We can easily find ourselves putting the Bible on a pedestal, even worshipping the book itself. As such, we may get upset when people disrespect the Bible by placing it on the ground or writing inside of it; we may even rigorously defend a particular translation of the Bible as the "correct" one. On the other hand, *Scripture as revealing authority* views the Bible as a dynamic story about God and his people that transforms us to live under and to live out of God's authority; it sees Scripture as a means to an end, the end being the revelation of God and his purposes.

We must remember that Jesus Christ is the Living Word (the *logos* we read about in John 1) who came in the flesh (incarnation) to reveal the Father to the world (John 14:6-11) and to provide believers with the

Holy Spirit as an Advocate (John 14:25-27; 16:7-15). Christ is, therefore, the authoritative revelation of the Triune God (Father, Son, and Holy Spirit). Scripture is authoritative in that it bears witness to God.[3] Our relationship must not be with a book, no matter how holy this Book is. Instead, we are called into a relationship with the living God, and Scripture, illuminated by the Holy Spirit, is the primary (but not the only) means by which we perceive, understand, and experience this God. If we are serious about relationship with God, we must be serious about spending time in God's Word and prayerfully and diligently seeking to understand what Scripture is communicating about God. We must also remember that it is not our human interpretations that are authoritative.

This last point is significant and should give us pause when asserting our own interpretation of any given passage of Scripture. In the words of the apostle Peter, "no prophecy of Scripture came about by the prophet's own interpretation of things" (2 Peter 1:20). When reading and interpreting Scripture, we must recognise the importance of several safeguards. First, the Holy Spirit is our guide as we seek to understand what God is revealing to us through the Word (1 Corinthians 2:10-16; cf. 2 Peter 1:21). For Christians, reading and interpreting the Bible is a spiritual activity, and the Spirit is able to help even the newest believers understand and apply the truths revealed.[4]

However, we also recognise that the Holy Spirit does not belong to any one individual but is given to the whole body of believers, the Church (Romans 8:1-17; 2 Corinthians 12:4-11). Therefore, second, the communion of saints (*communio sanctorum*)—past, present, and future—is another safeguard. We do not own the Holy Spirit, nor do we own the divine revelation. Therefore, we should invite others in the Christian community to evaluate, challenge, and confirm our readings of Scripture.

Third, Scripture is its own safeguard. Our interpretations should cohere with the picture of God that emerges from God's revelation in Christ as witnessed through the whole of Scripture. In this, we must remember that the books of the Bible were written over a large span of time and that the various contexts and experiences of the authors and their audiences resulted in diversity. Nevertheless, even in its multiplicity, there is a coherence in the overarching narrative concerning God and his activities.

The Inspiration of Scripture

The word *inspiration* comes from the Latin meaning "to breathe in." When we think about Scripture's inspiration, the words of 2 Timothy 3:16-17 often come to mind: "All Scripture is God-breathed (*theopneustos, meaning "breathed out"*) and is useful for teaching, rebuking, correcting and training in righteousness, so that the servant of God may be thoroughly equipped for every good work." When these words were written, they were in reference to the Old Testament Scriptures since much of the New Testament had not yet been written, and those books that had been written had not yet gained wide-spread authority within the church. Therefore, Paul's statement serves as a way of understanding the reality of God's inspiration of Scripture in general. However, it should not be used to argue that our current sixty-six books were divinely hand-written or to overemphasis Scripture's authority.

As Christians, the question we are seeking to answer is not whether or not the Bible is inspired; we believe this to be the case. Instead, we want to understand how God inspired the words of the Bible. There are several theories of inspiration that mostly differ with regard to the relationship between God and the human authors. On one side are views that significantly emphasise God's authorship. An extreme version of this stance is verbal dictation theory where the human writers were mere pens in the hand of the Divine. A more moderate stance, known as verbal plenary inspiration, sees the writers as being more personally involved in the process, while maintaining that they produced the exact words God wanted. On the other side, are views that place significant weight on the human authors. For example, intuition theory emphasises human insight and can refer more generally to the God-given inspiration of all people (sometimes called natural inspiration) or specifically to Christians (sometimes called spiritual illumination).[5]

A middle ground stance, known as dynamic theory of inspiration, holds that Scripture was inspired through a cooperative relationship between God and the human authors. God inspired human authors through the Holy Spirit to write out the biblical story in their own words and within their own historical and cultural situations. In the words of H. Orton Wiley, this view "maintains that the sacred writers were given extraordinary aid without any interference with their personal characteristics or activities. It preserves the scriptural truth that God speaks through human agencies, but insists that the agent is not reduced to a mere passive instrument."[6] This *does* mean that the various books of the Bible include a significant human element that *does not* always necessarily express the (full) views of God. One example may be seen in the apostle Paul's words found in 1 Corinthians 7:1-16, where he distinguishes multiple times between his own words and desires (verses 1-9 and 12-16) and the commands of God (verses 10-11).

Some Christians fear that such a view does not fully acknowledge God's power and may lessen Scripture's authority. However, this view has at least three strengths. First, it affirms what we know about God from Scripture itself. Scripture continually and consistently paints a picture of a relational God who involves humanity in the plan of redemption and restoration, and this view aligns perfectly with that portrait of God. This God creates humanity with free will, and after the Fall, this God extends free grace, which allows humanity to freely choose once again. Second, it helps us explain differences between biblical accounts that treat the same event, as well as, divergent theological perspectives between the various books of the Bible. That is to say, these variations are easily explained by taking into account the authors' differing perspectives, backgrounds, audiences, and purposes. Third, this view also helps explain historical, scientific, and grammatical discrepancies found in Scripture as well as human words and actions that appear contrary to God's nature (e.g. Galatians 5:12).

Inerrancy Versus Infallibility

On the surface, the words inerrancy and infallibility are synonyms. However, when the church applies them to the Bible, these words take on different meanings, which have often been a source of division. On the one hand, the term inerrancy means "without error" and has come to refer to Scripture as absolutely perfect, not just with regard to doctrines and ethics, but everything it addresses including history and science. People who hold such a view of Scripture tend to exert a lot of energy defending it against scientific and historical discoveries that appear to threaten its accuracy and thus its authority. In their view, the Bible is always the final authority on all matters. Anyone or anything that disagrees is not just questioning the Bible, they are questioning God.

On the other hand, the term infallibility means "absolutely trustworthy" and when used of Scripture means unfailing in effectiveness with regard to its purpose. As we can see, the scope of this concept is more limited. Proponents of this perspective believe that Scripture's primary purpose is to reveal God's identity and God's full plan of salvation, which includes humanity's relationship with God and its role in God's restoration plan. In these areas, God's Word is absolutely trustworthy and unfailing in effectiveness. However, in the words of Roger Olsen, *"If* the Bible contains some errors, some discrepancies, that do not affect its *power to transform lives through faith-filled communion with God*, that is not important."[7] Here, we should be reminded that it is Holy Spirit revealing God to us through Scripture that transforms lives and not the Bible itself.

We can now see a clear line of connection between the various terms that have been defined thus far. If inspiration equals the very words of God, then the Bible must be inerrant in all things, and is, therefore, the final authority; it is the final incarnation of God to humanity. However, if inspiration is dynamic, then although Scripture may evidence human elements that are not divine, it, nevertheless, is infallible, absolutely trustworthy concerning matters of salvation and perfectly revealing the authority of the Triune God.

The Church of the Nazarene's *Article of Faith* on Scripture states: "We believe in the plenary inspiration of the Holy Scriptures, by which we understand the 66 books of the Old and New Testaments, given by divine inspiration, inerrantly revealing the will of God concerning us in all things necessary to our salvation, so that whatever is not contained therein is not to be enjoined as an article of faith."[8] While a form of the word inerrant is used in this statement, it is significantly limited by its context.[9] Rather than using the adjectival form to describe Scripture itself (i.e., the inerrant Word of God), this statement uses the adverbial form to describe the dynamic action of how Scripture is without error in its "revealing the will of God concerning us in all things necessary to our salvation." In other words, the divine inspiration is limited in its effect to issues of salvation.

For some, this seems to limit Scripture's inspiration. However, this may be linked to a weak understanding of the doctrine of salvation (soteriology). Salvation is about so much more than just escaping hell. It encompasses, among other things, reconciliation with God, adoption into the body of Christ, infilling of the Holy Spirit, forgiveness of sin, and transformation into the image of God, what we might call discipleship and sanctification. In other words, salvation has as much to do with the present life as it has to do with the life to come.

Canon and Canonisation

Scripture is often referred to as the Canon, a word meaning "measuring rod" or "ruler." This terminology is connected to a process that took place in both Judaism and in early Christianity known as canonisation, which communities used to determine which books they recognised as authoritative. It is important to recognise two things here: first, this process took place over a long period of time; and second, there were multiple books available for consideration, many of which did not make it into the Canon.

What we know as the Old Testament is the Hebrew Bible or Hebrew Canon within Judaism. To be more precise, Jews use the term *Tanakh*, a word derived from the first letters of the three major sections: the *Torah*

(Teaching or Law); the *Nevi'im* (Prophets); and the *Khetuvim* (Writings). While the Hebrew Bible contains all the same books as the Protestant Old Testament, they are divided and ordered much differently, giving it a total of only twenty-four books rather than thirty-nine (see Figure 1).[10]

These books were written roughly between 1450 – 164 BC.[11] It is believed that canonisation took place in stages with the early Israelites

Tanakh (Hebrew Bible)	Protestant Canon
Torah	Pentateuch (or Law)
1. Genesis 2. Exodus 3. Leviticus 4. Numbers 5. Deuteronomy	1. Genesis 2. Exodus 3. Leviticus 4. Numbers 5. Deuteronomy
Nevi'im	Historical Books
6. Joshua 7. Judges 8. Samuel (1 & 2) 9. Kings (1 & 2) 10. Isaiah 11. Jeremiah 12. Ezekiel 13. The Book of the Twelve (which includes: Hosea, Joel, Amos, Obadiah, Jonah, Micah, Nahum, Habakkuk, Zephaniah, Haggai, Zechariah, Malachi)	6. Joshua 7. Judges 8. Ruth 9. 1 Samuel 10. 2 Samuel 11. 1 Kings 12. 2 Kings 13. 1 Chronicles 14. 2 Chronicles 15. Ezra 16. Nehemiah 17. Esther
Khetuvim	Wisdom Books
14. Psalms 15. Proverbs 16. Job 17. Song of Songs 18. Ruth 19. Lamentations 20. Ecclesiastes 21. Esther 22. Daniel 23. Ezra-Nehemiah 24 Chronicles (1 & 2)	18. Job 19. Psalms 20. Proverbs 21. Ecclesiastes 22. Song of Songs

	Prophets
	23. Isaiah
	24. Jeremiah
	25. Lamentations
	26. Ezekiel
	27. Daniel
	28. Hosea
	29. Joel
	30. Amos
	31. Obadiah
	32. Jonah
	33. Micah
	34. Nahum
	35. Habakkuk
	36. Zephaniah
	37. Haggai
	38. Zechariah
	39. Malachi

(FIGURE 1)

recognising the inspiration and authority of the *Torah* first, followed by the *Nevi'im*, and lastly the *Khetuvim*. However, we know very little about the actual process that took place. There does appear to have been continued debate among the Jewish rabbis, well into the first and second century AD, about the authority of a few books that are now found in the Hebrew Canon (e.g., Esther, Ecclesiastes, Song of Songs[12]). Still, as Roger Beckwith notes, "it is very striking that, over a period ranging from the second century BC (at latest) to the first century AD, so many writers, of so many classes (Semitic, Hellenistic, Pharisaic, Essene, Christian), show such agreement about the canon—agreement both with each other and with the present Hebrew Bible."[13] Indeed, the majority of the books of the Hebrew Bible, our Old Testament, are quoted or alluded to by the New Testament writings showing that Jesus and the early apostles recognised the authority of these books.[14]

Before moving to a discussion of New Testament canonisation, a word is in order about the *Old Testament Apocrypha*. The Roman Catholic Church and the various Eastern Orthodox churches (Greek, Russian,

Syrian, Ethiopian, etc.) have a different canon that includes a set of writing known as the Old Testament Apocrypha (Greek word meaning "hidden"). The Old Testament Apocrypha consists of around fifteen book (depending on how they are divided) that range in genre with most being either historical narrative/novel or wisdom literature. The Old Testament Apocrypha was part of some versions of the *Septuagint* (meaning seventy and often abbreviated with the Roman numerals LXX), which was the Greek translation of the Hebrew Scriptures. These books were never recognised as authoritative within Judaism and are not quoted in the New Testament.[15] However, many early Christian writings do make use of these books including Church Fathers such as Origen, Athanasius, and Augustine. Even John Wesley made use of some of these works, especially the Wisdom of Solomon and Sirach (also known as Ecclesiasticus).[16]

It was not until the time of the Reformation that Protestant Christians made a break from the Roman Catholic Church with regard to the Old Testament Apocrypha. It should also be noted that the Roman Catholic Church and Eastern Orthodox churches (as well as the Anglican and Episcopal Churches) view the Old Testament Apocrypha as Deutero-canonical, meaning "second canon," and do not believe they hold the same level of inspiration and authority as that of the rest of the Old Testament and New Testament. In the words of the Church Father Jerome, "the Church does read [the Apocrypha] for example of life and instruction of manners; but yet does not apply them to establish any doctrine."[17]

The twenty-seven books of the New Testament Canon (see Figure 2) were written roughly between 48-110 AD, and the process of canonisation was around 300 years in the making. Like with the Old Testament, the New Testament process of canonisation began organically as the worshipping community acknowledged the inspiration and authority of various books by their use of them in worship, discipleship, and writing. A set of early writings (1st and 2nd Century AD) that has come to be known as *The Apostolic Fathers*, which includes *1 Clement, 2 Clement, Ignatius, Polycarp, Didache, Barnabas, Shepherd of Hermas, Martyrdom of Polycarp*, and the *Epistle of Diognetus*, all make extensive use of most of the books

New Testament Canon				
Gospel	**History**	**Pauline Letters**	**General Letters**	**Apocalyptic**
1. Matthew 2. Mark 3. Luke 4. John	5. Acts	6. Romans 7. 1 Corinthians 8. 2 Corinthians 9. Galatians 10. Ephesians 11. Philippians 12. Colossians 13. 1 Thessalonians 14. 2 Thessalonians 15. 1 Timothy 16. 2 Timothy 17. Titus 18. Philemon	19. Hebrews 20. James 21. 1 Peter 22. 2 Peter 23. 1 John 24. 2 John 25. 3 John 26. Jude	27. Revelation

(FIGURE 2)

that would eventually become the New Testament. By the late second century (170-200 AD) a document known as the *Muratorian Canon* listed twenty-two of the New Testament book leaving out Hebrews, James, 1 & 2 Peter, and 3 John. It is not until 367 AD that Athanasius, Bishop of Alexandria, wrote a letter listing as authoritative the twenty-seven books as we have them today. The New Testament Canon was then more formally endorsed at the *Council of Hippo* (393 AD) and the *Council of Carthage* (397 AD).

Many may be surprised that a few of the New Testament books were disputed for so many years. Perhaps this is due to the time it took for these books to be circulated and become known throughout the church. Additionally, Hebrews was questioned because there was no author attached to this writing, and while the Apostle Paul was proposed, this was as much doubted then as it is today. James was disputed because of perceived contradiction with Paul over the issue of works versus grace; in actuality, there is no incongruity at all. The authorship of especially

21

2 Peter was scrutinised because of the significant differences in style from that of 1 Peter. And many of the shortest letters including 2 John, 3 John, and Jude were queried for their lasting value, since they were so brief.[18] It might also surprise some people that fourteen other books were considered for canonisation, which were finally rejected. Among the most noted were the *Shepherd of Hermas*, the *Epistle of Barnabas*, and the *Apocalypse of Peter*.[19]

As we can see, the process of canonisation of both the Old and New Testaments was a fluid endeavour that significantly involved the work of the Christian community. Scripture itself and the process of canonisation are part of the tradition of the church. Without the church, we do not have the Bible. From start to finish, the Bible is a partnership between God and his church. This should come as no surprise; this relational God has always involved humanity in his mission of redemption and restoration.

QUESTIONS FOR REFLECTION

1. What are some examples of people misusing the authority of Scripture?

2. Why is it important for us to invite others in the Christian community to evaluate, challenge, and confirm our readings of Scripture?

3. What do you see as the advantages and disadvantages of the various theories of inspiration? How do you see the dynamic theory of inspiration differing from the others?

4. What are the major difference between the concepts of inerrancy and infallibility when applied to the Bible? Why are these differences important?

5. Was there anything that surprised you about the process of canonisation? If so, what was it and why did it surprise you?

6. How does an understanding of God's relationality help us to understand some of the ideas presented in this chapter?

7. How would you explain your beliefs about Scripture to a non-believer? To a fellow believer?

CHAPTER 3

THE OLD TESTAMENT STORY OF GOD

Stories are important. They embrace us and move us. Stories connect us to one another. They remind us of our past and can teach us in our present. Stories can give us purpose and hope. They help us to embrace a larger picture. Whether we think about it in this way or not, our lives are a network of interconnected episodes that come together to present a picture of who we are. When our stories are combined with those of our family, our friends, or even our larger communities, they form a *grand narrative*, which can often help us to understand in greater depth individual episodes therein. The Bible is a prime example of this concept. Indeed, it is the grandest of narratives; it not only encompasses historic Israel and the historic church, it is a cosmic story that includes all of creation. As such, it provides insight into each of our stories. In the words of N. T. Wright, "We read scripture in order to be refreshed in our memory and understanding of the story within which we ourselves are actors, to be reminded where it has come from and where it is going to, and hence what our own part within it ought to be."[20]

It is a good reminder to us that, in God's grand narrative, we are the supporting actors and not the other way around. Likewise, the various characters portrayed in the books of the Bible (e.g., Abraham, Sarah, David, Esther, Isaiah, Mary, Paul) are also supporting actors. Humanity could not possibly encompass all of who God is and what he is doing in the world. However, as we locate ourselves within God's story, we find purpose and perspective. This purpose and perspective is born out of a proper understanding of who God is (Father, Son, and Holy Spirit) and what he has done, is doing, and will do. For this reason, we should read Scripture with the purpose of coming to know and understand this God at a deeper level. It is in the pages of Scripture that God's consistent character is revealed.

Read on a micro level, we quickly realise that the Bible contains many small episodes that differ considerably in their specifics while sharing some common aspects. If we are attentive, we may recognise a reoccurring scheme that goes something like this: God's invitation to relationship, human disobedience and its consequences, God's renewed engagement that results in renewed devotion and deliverance. Read from a macro level, we can say that the biblical story has a beginning (Creation), a conflict (the Fall), a plot (God's calling Israel to fulfil his mission), a climax (the Christ event), a continued plot (God's calling the Church to fulfil his mission), and a resolution (Christ's Second Coming, restoration and re-creation). Both levels are important and give us insight to engage Scripture at a theological level, which helps us to better understand God and apply this knowledge to our lives and to our context. We can call this theological level the *Big Picture* as it seeks to understand and answer the following three questions:

1. What do we learn about the character of God?
2. What do we learn about God's plans for all creation?
3. What do we learn about our role in the unfolding story?

Here, we are unable to do a comprehensive study of each biblical book. Instead, we have divided the Bible up into larger groupings that share common, overarching themes and briefly highlighted some of the main points of response to the three Big Picture questions. Hopefully, this summary will become a springboard for deeper study and interaction with God's grand narrative. In this chapter, we cover the Old Testament and in the next chapter the New Testament.

The God Who Creates (Genesis 1–11)

The opening chapters of Genesis are significant and provide the structure for the rest of God's unfolding story. Therein, we quickly come to see that this God is the *God who creates* everything and everyone (all other debates that surround Genesis 1 and 2 are secondary). Creation is not just something this God did; it is core to who he is—God is life and God is light. In the words of John 1:3-4, "All things came into being through him, and without him not one thing came into being. What has come into being in him was life, and the life was the light of all people" (NRSV). In other words, God defines what life is and genuine life is only found in him. Furthermore, all humanity has been created in the image and likeness of this God (Genesis 1:26-27) and contains God's breath of life (Genesis 2:7).

This leads us to one of the most pressing and profound questions concerning life: Why are we here? The answer is simple: because God wanted to be in relationship with us. Not only is God life and light, God is love (1 John 4:8, 16). We Wesleyans believe that love is God's primary attribute and chief characteristic. Everything else God is or is not is defined by his love; this includes his sovereignty. This means that God creates out of love and because of love. He is a relational God.[21] This brings light to our own nature; we are relational beings. We were created in God's image and whatever else this image of God (*imago Dei*) may mean for humanity, it includes relationality (cf. Genesis 2:18; 5:3).

God's love for humanity and desire for genuine relationship means that he created us with free will. Adam and Eve were not forced into relationship with God; they were given a choice, one which included the possibility for disobedience. The story of the Fall evidences this reality. God gave Adam and Eve dominion over all the creatures of the earth (Genesis 1:26-30; 2:15-20), but they elevated a creature over the Creator by taking the serpent's word as truer than God's (Genesis 3:5). In other words, the first sin was one of idolatry, of putting someone or something above God and of distorting the created order and the divine relationship between humanity and God (cf. Romans 1:18-32). Still, even in the midst of human disobedience, God showed mercy and continued to reach out in love to humanity in the hopes that humanity would recognise who he truly was, would come to trust in him, and would reflect him in the world.

While sin had consequences (Genesis 3:14-24), not least of which was a break down in relationship, God reached out with free grace making it possibly for humanity to choose him once more. Despite this, the story of humanity is one of continued sin and continued estrangement from God. The narrative of Genesis 3–11 can quite accurately be described as a downward spiral into greater disobedience and greater separation from God. What started out with the violation of a command of God quickly escalated into murder (Genesis 4), total corruption of humanity (Genesis 6–9), and the attempt by humanity to make a name for itself without God (Genesis 11). Nevertheless, where sin reigned, God's love reigned mightier. This is witnessed in God's engagement in conversation with Adam and Eve after the Fall, with Cain after his murder of Abel, in God's choosing of Noah, his rainbow covenant after the flood, and even in God's confusing of languages and scattering of the peoples. This God is serious about creating, recreating, and restoring relationship! This is the story from the beginning and continues to be the story throughout all of Scripture and throughout all of human history.

To summarise, we learned that our God is the God who creates, and that this creation take place out of God's deep and expansive love; in other words, creativeness is an extension of his core nature of love. We have learned that God's plan includes ongoing relationship with humanity, who are invited to join God in the process of creating and recreating. Finally, we learned that our role in God's unfolding story is to recognise who he is, to walk in genuine relationship with him, and to reflect him to our world.

The God Who Calls (Genesis 12 – Exodus)

That this God is the *God who calls* is not surprising to those familiar with the biblical stories. There are numerous examples of God calling people into relationship and mission with him. Abraham's and Moses's callings are among the most significant as they represent God's choice of the people of Israel and entering into covenant with them. A covenant was a "solemnly sworn commitment, guaranteeing promises or obligations undertaken by one or both covenanting parties."[22] If either party did not uphold its part of the agreement, then the covenant was broken and there could be significant consequences, especially for the weaker party member.

These types of conditional covenants were quite common in the contexts and cultures of the biblical world. What made most of the covenants between God and humanity unique was, that at their core, they were unconditional. Abram was called to go to a new land (Genesis 12:1), the male Israelites were called to be circumcised (Genesis 17:9-14), Moses was called to confront Pharaoh and to lead the people to the promised land (Exodus 3:10), and Israel was called to keep God's commands (Exodus 19:5). Nevertheless, their decisions to participate did not determine whether God's promises would come to fruition. It usually did determine whether or not those involved would be included in the blessings and also changed the particulars of how God would fulfil his promises. Still, God was committed to the fulfillment of his overarching purpose of making himself known to all the nations, blessing them, and redeeming and restoring all of creation. God was simple inviting Israel to participate in this blessing of others (Genesis 12:3; 22:18), just as he continues to invite all current believers to participate in the *missio Dei* (mission of God).

There are several aspects of God's calling upon people that are bewildering. First, God includes humanity in his redemptive plans, even as he knows they will reject, disobey, and fail. Second, he does not force participation; each person is invited to choose to accept the invitation and then daily to choose to faithfully walk this journey. Third, God continues to pursue humanity even as humanity continues to reject, to disobey, and to fail. Fourth, God invites dynamic and honest interaction within the relationship. This final point is seen, for example, in Abraham being allowed to question God's intentions toward Sodom (Genesis 18:22-33), in Jacob being allowed to wrestle with God (Genesis 32:22-32), in Moses being allowed to doubt God's selection of him as an appropriate leader for the task at hand (Exodus 3:10–4:17), and especially in Moses being able to argue with God to the point that God "changed his mind" about destroying Israel (Exodus 32:7-14).

All these points appear to add up to a fairly unimpressive God, at least from a worldly perspective. Yet, they are proof that this God is not like the many other gods that we tend to construct in our own image, which are usually based on human lust for power. Instead, the true God, while possessing all power and knowledge, is pure love and desires relationship more than blind obedience. This is why our primary calling is not to some task but to genuine relationship with God and others.

The relationality of God is seen in the Ten Commandments (Exodus 20:1-17; Deuteronomy 5:6-21) and in the tabernacle (Exodus 25–31). The Ten Commandments provided Israel with guidelines for living in relationship with God (commandments 1-4) and others (commandments 5-10). Thus, Jesus could easily sum up the Greatest Commandment in the words: "Love the Lord your God with all your heart and with all your soul and with all your mind" (cf. Deuteronomy 6:4) and "Love your neighbour as yourself" (cf. Leviticus 19:18), and he could add that, "All the Law and the Prophets hang on these two commandments" (Matthew 22:37-40). Additionally, the tabernacle signified the presence of God in the midst of the community, and his willingness to go with them on their journey toward the promised land.

To summarise, we learned that the God who calls, does so out of his desire to restore broken relationship; in other words, calling is an extension of God's loving nature. Furthermore, we learned that God's relationality means that he is determined to include humanity in his plan of reconciliation and restoration, and that he will continue to call humanity back into relationship and will continue to call humanity into mission. Finally, we are reminded that our role is to walk in trust and obedience, which can only take place as we embrace the call to genuine relationship with God and others, and as we come to accept the *missio Dei* as our own calling.

The God Who Provides (Leviticus – Joshua)

As the biblical narrative unfolds, it becomes obvious that God sought to reveal himself to Israel and to help them understand the kind of God he was. Therein, the people learned that he was the *God who provides*, both in the things he provided and the ways he provided. In Leviticus we learn that God is *holy*, and that this holiness was meant to extend to the people—"Be holy because I, the Lord your God, am holy" (Leviticus 19:2). While some simply see this as an unattainable command, it can also be understood as: (1) a declaration of God's nature; and (2) an invitation to have our nature transformed by his. In other words, this God desires such intimate relationship with humanity that he provides a way to reverse the brokenness and make humanity whole and holy, both as individuals and as a community. We further learn that holiness involves care for the neighbour that is like us, and care for the neighbour that is not like us—the "alien" (Leviticus 19:33-34; cf. Luke 10:29-37). God desires the reconciliation and restoration of human relationships, one to the other, and while holiness is ultimately determined by our relationship with God, this holiness is manifested and maintained in relationship with others.

The initial provision for this holiness comes through the sacrificial system. For many people today, the sacrificial system seems barbaric and unnecessary. However, within the cultural milieu of the Israelites, this system provided them with a familiar way to worship and honour their God. The sacrificial system reveals that God is willing to meet humanity where they are rather than expecting humanity to meet him where he is. Nevertheless, in its familiarity, there was unfamiliarity. The sacrificial system constructed for Israel was much different from that of the surrounding nations. For example, other groups sacrificed human children (Deuteronomy 12:31; Psalm 106:38), were involved in self-mutilation (1 Kings 18:28), and even believed their offerings fed the gods[23] (cf. Psalm 50:12-14). Additionally, the reason for their sacrifices were usually to appease the gods or to sway these gods toward some particular blessing (e.g., victory in war, good harvest, children).

Israel's sacrificial system included five different kinds of sacrifices, three of which were voluntary (*burnt offering, grain offering,* and *peace offering*), allowing Israel to acknowledge general human sinfulness, to express devotion and thanksgiving to God, and to celebrate special occasions (Leviticus 1–3). The final two offering types dealt with transgressions. The *sin offering* was aimed at providing purification, atonement, and forgiveness for sins of omission and unintentional mistakes (Leviticus 4:1–5:13). Similarly, the *burnt offering* provided atonement and forgiveness from the guilt incurred by sin, both unintentional and intentional, and included restitution of damages plus twenty percent of the value (Leviticus 5:14–6:7). Additionally, the *Day of Atonement* (Leviticus 16; 23:26-32; Numbers 29:7-11), which was considered the holiest of days, provided for corporate atonement and forgiveness. As we examine the various offerings, we see that they are really for the people and not for God (cf. Isaiah 1:10-15). The sacrificial system provided the people with a means of honouring God and maintaining their relationship with him. It also enabled them to live in harmony with their neighbours by making restitution for their wrongs. It gave the people a way to participate in the life of God and the life of the community.

This God of provision gave sustenance to Israel as they wandered through the desert (Exodus 16:1–17:7; Numbers 11:31-34), and ultimately provided them with the promised land of Canaan. This land was significant not simply because it was "a land flowing with milk and honey" (Exodus 3:8; Joshua 5:6). Its strategic location bridged the Mediterranean lands to the north and south. It provided Israel with the opportunity to bear witness to the holiness of God in the way they lived and worshipped. Nevertheless, in spite of all God's provisions, Israel continued to struggle with disobedience.

To summarise, we learned that God's provision is ultimately about extending his relational invitation to humanity. In other words, God's provision is an extension of his love and desire for humanity to engage him in genuine relationship. We also learned that God is a holy God and that this holiness is extended to humanity. Part of God's plan for his creation is restoration, which means more than just deliverance. It means transformation into a holy people who extend this holiness into the world. We are called to allow God to transform us individually and corporately into a holy people and to become God's provision to others that they might come to know, worship, and reflect this God as well.

The God Who Accommodates (Judges – 2 Chronicles)

It may seem odd to refer to God as the *God who accommodates*. The act of accommodating includes an element of provision and mercy, but, more-over, it includes the adaptation or adjustment on God's part to meet the people where they are, usually in the midst of their sinfulness or mis-aligned desires. Thus, this moniker is fitting, and reveals the extent of God's patience towards Israel for the sake of ongoing relationship. The book of Judges provides a good snapshot of Israel's continuous cycle of disobedience. As each new generation rose they forgot about God's good deeds, abandoned God, returned to their evil ways, and served other gods (cf. Judges 2:10-11). This turning led to military loss, death, and destruction, at which point they cried out to God, who raised up a leader (often called a "judge") to deliver Israel and restore her to relationship with God.[24] These judges were part of God's accommodation. In other words, they were not the ideal. They were a kind of acquiescence on God's part.

Israel's demand for an earthly king was another act of God's accom-modating.[25] Israel wanted a king so that she could be like all the other nations. God's response to a distressed Samuel was revealing—"Listen to all that the people are saying to you; it is not you they have rejected, but they have rejected me as their king" (1 Samuel 8:7). God's adjustment came with a strong warning about all that an earthly king would cost Israel (1 Samuel 8:11-18; cf. Deuteronomy 17:14-20), which was mostly fulfilled by the time of Solomon's reign (1 Kings 11:1-13; 2 Chronicles 1–9), and which resulted in a divided kingdom (1 King 12). God had established a theocracy, but the people wanted a monarchy. They were in constant need of a physical representation of God in their midst. However, this human representative most often resulted in the people forgetting that God was their one true King, "high and exalted, seated on a throne" (Isaiah 6:1).

God also accommodated Israel with the Temple. King David's desire to build God a permanent dwelling place was met with these words: "I have not dwelt in a house from the day I brought the Israelites up out of Egypt to this day. I have been moving from place to place with a tent as my dwelling. Wherever I have moved with all the Israelites, did I ever say to any of their rulers whom I commanded to shepherd my people Israel, 'Why have you not built me a house of cedar?'" (2 Samuel 7:6-7). Like the role of a king, a temple helped to establish the stability and significance of a people; it showed their connection to and support from the divine.[26] David's desire to build a Temple for God and Solomon's completion of this dream was as much about establishing a centralised location for governance and military in order to unite a kingdom as it was about wanting God to have a suitable dwelling place (cf. 2 Chronicles 2:1; 7:11). In some respects, it was an attempt to control God's comings and goings. While eventually allowing such a Temple to be built, God reminded Solomon that his presence would only remain as long as Solomon and the people humbled themselves, prayed, sought God's face, and turned from their wicked ways (2 Chronicles 7:12-22). Furthermore, God reminded David that it was God who would establish David's house rather than the other way around (2 Samuel 7:11-16; cf. Psalm 89), which was a foreshadowing of God's messianic provision of Christ.

To summarise, throughout these narratives, we see God's patience and grace. In the midst of human sin and human longings, God accommodates these people with Judges, Kings, and a Temple, even though these were not part of his original plan. Why? Because God knows the depths of the Fall and the power of culture, and because he is determined to walk in relationship with this people. We learned that the details of God's plans were flexible, but he was resolute in his overarching purpose of redemption and restoration. This plan was ultimately grounded in Christ but continued to include faithful humanity. We also learned that we must continue to grow in our understanding of who this God is and what his plan is. This will often require us to move beyond our own desires and even our own cultural comforts to ask whether they align with the character and mission of God. Furthermore, God's accommodation should encourage us to be more accommodating (patient) toward others who are at different points in their life and faith journey.

The God Who Wrestles (Job – Song of Songs, Lamentations)

This is perhaps the strangest of all the monikers we have explored. Nevertheless, in light of what we know about Israel, and about ourselves, it should not surprise us that we serve the *God who wrestles* and the God who invites wrestling. We have already made brief mention of Jacob's wrestling with God (Genesis 32:22-32), but we have yet to explore the full implication of this story. As a result of this wrestling match, Jacob (meaning "deceiver" or "cheater") became Israel (meaning "the one who struggles/strives/wrestles with God"), and Jacob's story represented Israel's story (and humanity's) as a whole. Throughout the Bible, God demonstrated that he was not afraid to roll up his proverbial sleeves and get dirty for the sake of honest and genuine relationship, and he invited the people of Israel to do the same. In spite of their continued disobedience, if Israel continued to engage God and wrestle with him, then he would continue to wrestle with them.

The story of Job is another example of such relational wrestling. As we read through this book we are taken aback by Job's strong accusations toward God—"I say to God: Do not declare me guilty, but tell me what charges you have against me. Does it please you to oppress me, to spurn the work of your hands, while you smile on the plans of the wicked ... though you know that I am not guilty and that no one can rescue me from your hand?" (Job 10:3, 7). Job, like his "friends," was mistaken about God. But what set Job apart from the others, who were reprimanded for their words, was that Job actually engaged God head on, and in return, God engaged Job head on as well (Job 38–41).[27]

The most prevalent example of God's allowance of human wrestling is found is the Psalms of lament, which make up more than a third of the Psalms. These laments were written on behalf of individuals or a whole community, and reveal a plethora of deep emotions including grief, anger, frustration, and doubt. In each case, God allowed humanity to cry out in its pain before a listening God—"How long, Lord? Will you forget me forever? How long will you hide your face from me?" (Psalm 13:1); "You have rejected us, God, and burst upon us; you have been angry—now restore us!" (Psalm 60:1). The laments provided a structure "to move a worshipper from hurt to joy, from darkness to light, from desperation to hope."[28] Ultimately, they offered a means for expressing trust in God in the midst of his seeming absence—"But I trust in your unfailing love; my heart rejoices in your salvation. I will sing the Lord's praise, for he has been good to me" (Psalm 13:5-6); "With God we will gain the victory, and he will trample down our enemies" (Psalm 22:12).

The book of Psalms in not alone in its cries of lament. They are heard in various places throughout the Old Testament. The whole of Lamentations is a book of pain, recognising the consequences of sin and pleading to God for mercy. It is a reminder to us that "grief is not a private matter. The author challenges us to openly speak about our agony and pain and the chaos that surrounds our human existence."[29] One of the greatest aspects of the Wisdom Literature (Job, Proverbs, and Ecclesiastes) and the Songs of the Community (Psalms, Song of Songs, and Lamentations) is that they testify to the collective wisdom of multiple generations who come together to share in the joys and struggles of life before God. They remind us that God is not afraid of our questions and doubts, not even our anger, as long as it comes as part of the pursuit of honest and genuine relationship.

To summarise, we recognised the depths of God's love, his willingness to engage humanity in a wrestling match for the sake of genuine relationship. Similarly, God desires that humanity reciprocate this honest engagement with him. In other words, the relationship between God and humanity is not designed to be one of master and servant, but one of mutual friendship, while still recognising the authority of God (see John 15:12-17). Such relationship requires us to be open and honest with God; he invites wrestling. We are called to engage God with all of who we are, to cry out to him in both the good and the bad times. We are also called to genuinely engage others and share in this journey together.

The God Who Delivers (Isaiah – Malachi, Ezra – Esther)

For many people, the primary way of understanding God is as the *God who delivers*. Nevertheless, this deliverance is often viewed too narrowly. Israel also struggled at points with a view of God's deliverance that was too narrow, which excluding those not like them. Although Israel was called to be a blessing to the nations (Genesis 12:3; 22:18), their disobedience led to the profaning of God's name among the nations (Ezekiel 36) and led to their own destruction and exile (2 Chronicles 36:15-21). Through the prophets, God reminded Israel of his love for all creation (e.g., Jonah) and of his desire to bless the nations through Israel's obedience (e.g., Jeremiah 4:1-2; Zechariah 8:13).

As we read through the prophets, it is important to note the difference between predictive and prescriptive prophecy. Most people are familiar with predictive prophecy, which foretells in the present the certainty of future events. Nevertheless, most biblical prophecy is prescriptive, declaring actions that are in line with the character of God and the historic revelation of God's activity; it is forth-telling. "The prophets are not inspired to make any points or announce any doctrines that are not already contained in the Pentateuchal covenant."[30] The prophets' proclamations are a continual reminder to Israel of her disobedience and of the most likely outcome of such disobedience. It forced Israel to remember God's covenant and God's character.

When the people remembered God and cried out to him, God did listen and eventually did deliver. However, this liberation did not take place as quickly as the people hoped. The people were often warned against false prophets who were filling them with false hopes (e.g., Jeremiah 23:16; Micah 3:11), proclaiming Israel's immediate release. Instead, in the midst of their exile, God continued to invite Israel to fulfil her calling to bless the other nations, even her captors—"seek the peace and prosperity of the city to which I have carried you into exile. Pray to the Lord for it, because if it prospers, you too will prosper" (Jeremiah 29:7).

God's historic deliverance of Israel often came through unlikely "servants." Deliverance from Babylon took place through King Cyrus of Persia (Isaiah 45:1-7). Cyrus not only released Israel from exile, he passed down the charge from God to rebuild the Temple in Jerusalem and returned the treasure that king Nebuchadnezzar had stolen from the original Temple (Ezra 1). Esther, a young Jewish orphan who was adopted by her cousin Mordecai, was perhaps the most improbable deliverer. She risked her life and used her newfound position as queen of Persia to save all the Jewish people from genocide (Esther 8). Finally, God also worked through King Artaxerxes of Persia to release Nehemiah to rebuild the wall around Jerusalem (Nehemiah 2).

God's deliverance was not limited to Israel (e.g., Nineveh), nor was it limited to a specific time in history. Throughout the prophetic writings, we see glimpses of a more complete and cosmic salvation—an everlasting redemption of all of creation. Amos's words about the great and terrible Day of the Lord (Amos 5:18-20; cf. Isaiah 2) developed into an eschatological (pertaining to last things) concept (Zephaniah 3:11-13; Malachi 4:5:6), one which the early church believed was inaugurated in the person of Christ at his first coming. Indeed, the church came to understand Christ as the true Suffering Servant of Isaiah 40–55, who "poured out his life unto death, ... bore the sin of many, and made intercession for the transgressors" (Isaiah 53:12). There are many other phenomena connected to God's eschatological redemption: Jeremiah spoke of God's establishment of a New Covenant, where the law was written on humanity's hearts (Jeremiah 31:33-34); Joel spoke about a day when God's Spirit would be poured out on all flesh (Joel 2:28-29; cf. Ezekiel 37:1-14); Isaiah spoke about the creation of a New Heaven and New Earth where there would be no more weeping and where the wolf and lamb would feed together (Isaiah 65:17-25; 66:22-23); and Daniel spoke of a coming King who would have an everlasting Kingdom (Daniel 7:9-28). It is also important to note, in each of these phenomena, God's people are called to actively participate in God's deliverance and restoration.

To summarise, we saw that humanity's sin and disobedience has lasting consequences, not least of which is separation from God and his promises. Thankfully, we also learned that God is the great deliverer and that his deliverance is connected to his love and covenant faithfulness. Furthermore, we learned that God's plan of deliverance includes both the present and the future (eschatological deliverance), both humanity and the whole of creation. Throughout, we seen that God's deliverance includes human participation, first in our remembrance of God and trust in him, then in our extension of God's deliverance and restoration in this world.

QUESTIONS FOR REFLECTION

1. How important are stories in your particular cultural context? Have you ever thought of the Bible in terms of a grand narrative? How do you see God's story and your own story (or the story of your church) intersecting?

2. How does the reality of God as creator shape the way you view humanity and humanity's desire to create?

3. What do you see as God's calling on your life? What is the calling of your local church? How does God's story shape these various callings?

4. How has God provide for you personally, for your family, your church? How has this provision helped you to be holy, and allowed you to worship him more?

5. What are your thoughts concerning the idea that God accommodates us for the sake of relationship? How has God accommodated you and your church? What can you learn from this?

6. Have you ever "wrestled" with God? What was the reason and what was the outcome? What does this teach us about God and his desire for genuine relationship?

7. In what ways does your (or your church's) view of God's deliverance need to be expanded?

CHAPTER 4

THE NEW TESTAMENT STORY OF GOD

For many Christians, the Old Testament is at best foreign and at worst completely irrelevant; some people even view the Old Testament as antithetical to the New Testament. Such a view is unfortunate since, in reality, the New Testament is the continuation of the Old Testament. As such, the meaning and significance of the New Testament is more fully revealed when read in the light of the Old Testament. It is as we read these two testaments together that we see the fullness of God's love as evidenced in God's actions from start to finish, from promise to fulfilment.

The God Who Comes (Matthew – Luke)

"She will give birth to a son, and you are to give him the name Jesus, because he will save his people from their sins. ... The virgin will conceive and give birth to a son, and they will call him Immanuel (which means 'God with us')" (Matthew 1:21, 23). These words are a clear reminder to us that we serve a *God who comes*! In the person of Jesus of Nazareth, "The Word became flesh and made his dwelling among us" (John 1:14). The incarnation is profound evidence of God's love for humanity and shows the lengths he will go to restore the human race. In the incarnation, "God is recreating our humanity"; "God and man meet in Jesus Christ and a new covenant is eternally established and fulfilled."[31]

Jesus's incarnation also inaugurated the Kingdom of God or Kingdom of Heaven (these terms are interchangeable). In Jewish understanding, the Kingdom of God did not pertain to a location as such, but to the reign of the King. Whenever and wherever the sovereignty of God was acknowledged, and his rule accepted, there was the Kingdom. While the Jews knew that God reigned supreme at all times, they believed that a day would come when every knee would bow, and every tongue would confess this reality (Isaiah 45:23; Romans 14:11; Philippians 2:10-11). This is also why Jesus taught his disciples to pray "your kingdom come, your will be done, on earth as it is in heaven" (Matthew 6:10). The Kingdom of God is an eschatological reality that is both present and future.

It was already noted that eschatology pertains to the study of last things. Unfortunately, this concept has often been relegated to a simple doctrine concerning the Second Coming of Christ and the "End Times." Nevertheless, it is so much more than this. More than an event it is a worldview, which is woven throughout the fabric of the Old and New Testament as well as throughout much of the early Jewish writings. This worldview understands time as temporal and linear, having a definite beginning and moving toward a definite end. In this way, all of creation has purpose. This worldview also holds a cosmic perspective, believing that God's actions and human participation encompasses the fate of the whole created order. Finally, an eschatological worldview is centred on God's redemption and restoration of his creation and the salvation and transformation of God's people.

Jesus came as the long-expected Messiah ("anointed one"), and ushered in the eschatological age, the beginning of the Day of the Lord. But his messiahship did not live up to the expectations of many, who wanted a political or military leader to overthrow Rome and establish Israel's dominance among the nations. In other words, the messianic age was supposed to mean deliverance for the people of God and divine judgment for the nations who had opposed God and his people. Since "Messiah" had so many expectations tied to it, Jesus employed the title "Son of Man" to refer to himself (e.g., Matthew 9:6; Mark. 8:31; Luke 9:22). This title was likely borrowed from Daniel 7:13-14 and allowed

Jesus to define his own messiahship as a suffering servant who would "give his life as a ransom for many" (Mark 10:45), which echoed the language and imagery of Isaiah 52:13–53:12 (cf. Matthew 26:28). Through Jesus's death and resurrection, he overcame sin and death, becoming an atoning sacrifice (Romans 3:25). In the words of Hebrews 9:28, "Christ was sacrificed once to take away the sins of many; and he will appear a second time, not to bear sin, but to bring salvation to those who are waiting for him." Jesus's first coming was focused on seeking and saving the lost (Luke 19:10); it was marked by grace, love, justice, healing, and self-sacrifice. This singular focus confused many, including the religious leaders, even John the Baptist (Matthew 11:2-6), as did Jesus's teaching on his Second Coming. This is because the Jewish view of time and history was completely linear (see Figure 3).

Jewish View of Time and History

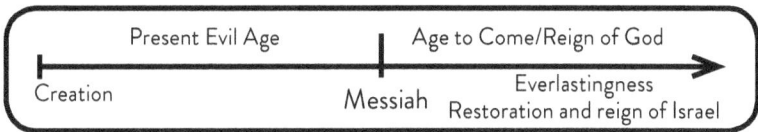

(FIGURE 3)

Jesus introduced a hiccup in the timeline, what we might call the "time between the times" (see Figure 4). This is the space in which we live as the eschatological church. *Already* the Kingdom of God is present, but it is *not yet* evident to all. We *already* experience God's salvation, and with it, God's transformation, but we do *not yet* enjoy its fulness. Here, in the midst of the *already* and *not yet*, we as the church are invited to participate in the *missio Dei*, helping others to experience God's salvation, and with it, God's emerging Kingdom. We are invited to incarnate Christ in our world by living out the Great Commandment of love for God and neighbour (Matthew 22:37-40), and by embracing the Great Commission of making Christlike disciples in our world (Matthew 28:19-20).

Jesus's View of Time and History

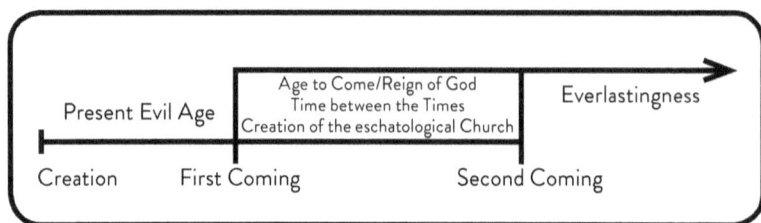

(FIGURE 4)

To summarise, we saw how Christ's incarnation, along with his life, death, and resurrection, was the greatest evidence of God's love. We learned that God comes into the world, becoming human, in order to break the grip of sin upon creation and to show humanity a better way to live in full communion and union with God. Furthermore, Christ's death and resurrection provided a means of atonement and began the process of bringing the fullness of the Kingdom of God here on earth. We are called to be incarnational, putting on Christ, living amongst hurting people, and showing them the love and salvation of Christ in tangible ways.

The God Who Dwells (John – Acts)

God's dwelling *among* his people is not new; we have seen it from the beginning. However, the reality of God dwelling *within* his people is radical and proves that he is the *God who dwells*. While there were occasions in the Old Testament when God's Spirit temporarily came upon a person who had been chosen for a particular tasks (e.g. Exodus 31:2-3; Judges 3:10; Isaiah 11:2), it was the exception, not the rule. God's people looked forward to a day when God would permanently pour out the Holy Spirit upon all his people, male and female, young and old, slave and freeperson (Joel 2:28-29). This dream was realised through the death, resurrection, and ascension of Christ.

The book of Acts recounts the coming of the Holy Spirit upon believers at Pentecost. Having been filled with the Spirit, believers began to speak in other languages, so that those present heard the words in their native tongue (Acts 2:4-12). This episode has been described by some as a reversal of the Babel story (Genesis 11:1-9), as it brings together languages.[32] However, the problem with Babel was not the common language, but that the people did not want to be "scattered over the face of the whole earth" (Genesis 11:4); they were ignoring God's earlier command for humanity to fill the earth with God's glory (Genesis 1:28; 9:1; cf. Isaiah 11:9; Habakkuk 2:14).[33] On the other hand, Acts is structured around Jesus's commission to scatter the message of Christ abroad— "But you will receive power when the Holy Spirit comes on you; and you will be my witnesses in Jerusalem, and in all Judea and Samaria, and to the ends of the earth" (Acts 1:8). Through the power of the Holy Spirit the church is enabled to live out the mission of God in the world. Being Christ's "witnesses," in word and deed, becomes a core part of the church's identity.[34]

A significant part of this witness was the unity of this first community. "All the believers were together and had everything in common" (Acts 2:44); they were "one in heart and mind" (Acts 4:32). This group was actively living out the Great Commandment and the Great Commission, and as a result, "the Lord added to their number daily those who were being saved" (Acts 2:47). Their sharing in the same Spirit enabled them to put the other above themselves (cf. Philippians 2:1-4), to tangibly evidence the fruit of the Spirit (Galatians 5:22-23), and to use their spiritual gifts to build up the body of Christ (1 Corinthians 12:4-11; Ephesians 4:1-16). The indwelling of the Holy Spirit in the life of the church makes the ordinary extraordinary; the Spirit builds us into a singular, holy temple of God in our world (1 Corinthians 3:16-17).

In the Gospel of John, Jesus spoke about the sending of the *Paraclete*, a Greek word often translated as "advocate," "helper," "counsellor," or "companion"; it is more literally rendered "one who is called alongside." The role of the *Paraclete* or "Spirit of truth" is to abide in the believer, uniting them to God (John 14:17, 20); to teach the believer "all things" (John 14:26; 16:12-14); to give the believe peace (John 14:27); to testify about Jesus, especially through the believer (John 15:26-27); and to convince the world about sin, righteousness, and judgment (16:8-11). In

ENGAGING THE STORY OF GOD

many respects, the Holy Spirit does internally what Jesus did externally while present with his disciples (cf. 1 John 2:1).

Another important teaching on the Holy Spirit is found in Romans 8. Therein, Paul highlights the following points: the "law of the Spirit" makes the decisive difference in setting us free from "the law of sin and death" (verses 1-2); believers are those "who live in accordance with the Spirit" and therefore have the same mind and desire as the Spirit (verses 5-6); only those with the Spirit belong to Christ (verse 9); the Spirit brings true resurrection life to the Christian in the present and helps us to overcome sin (verses 10-13); the Spirit marks membership into the family of God making us co-heirs with Christ (verses 14-17); the Spirit is the first-fruits of complete salvation where at the end of this age we will experience the redemption of our bodies (verses 23-25); and the Spirit aids us in our weakness, by interceding for us "in accordance with the will of God" (verses 26-27).

To summarise, we learned that God's dwelling in us is a deepening of his dwelling among us, which is an extension of his love for us and a recognition of our need for intimacy, guidance, and love. We learned that God's desire is not just to save us, but to transform us, both individually and corporately, making us into a holy people who reflect the *imago Dei* in our world. Our calling is to embrace this dwelling, to allow the Holy Spirit to transform us, unite us, teach us, and use us to reveal Christ to others. In the words of G. R. Beasley-Murray, "the church, commissioned and authorized by the Risen Lord, is renewed by the Holy Spirit to pursue its mission to the world in his holy fellowship. The glory of Christ in his death-resurrection-exaltation is revealed through the church by the ever-present aid of the Holy Spirit."[35]

The God Who Gathers (Romans – Jude)

Throughout God's story, we have seen, time and time again, his love for all people and every nation. In the person of Christ, and through the work of the Holy Spirit, the early church was a firsthand witness to the initial fulfillment of Isaiah's words: "The Sovereign Lord declares—he who gathers the exiles of Israel: 'I will gather still others to them besides those already gathered'" (Isaiah 56:8; cf. Isaiah 2:1). The reality of Gentiles coming to faith in Christ and being filled with the Holy Spirit was proof that the eschatological age had come, and that God was indeed the God who gathers "from every nation, tribe, people and language" (Revelation 7:9).

The conversion of Paul to Christ-follower and his calling to be an apostle to the Gentiles (Galatians 1:11-24; Acts 26:12-18) was a significant part of God's plan to reveal himself to the nations. An insider at the highest echelons of power within Judaism had moved from persecutor to promotor of the Gospel of Christ, from legalistic purity to radical defender of those once deemed unclean. Paul's missionary journeys saw many Gentiles come to faith in Christ apart from works of the law, which in turn nearly divided the young church. It was at the Jerusalem Council (Acts 15:1-35; Galatians 2:1-10) that Paul and Barnabas joined the leaders in Jerusalem to debate the validity of a law-free mission to the Gentiles. There it was agreed that God was doing a new work among the nations that must not be hindered by forcing Gentiles to maintain Jewish standards of law observance.

Paul was not alone in his work among the nations. Peter ministered to both Jews and Gentiles (Acts 10–11), and 1 Peter was likely written to a predominately Gentile audience,[36] who were described as "God's elect, exiles scattered throughout" (1 Peter 1:1). This was not just an issue of nationality. One of the most radical examples of God's gathering grace is found in the story of Philip and the Ethiopian eunuch (Acts 8:26-39). Various Old Testament laws prohibited eunuchs from becoming priests (Leviticus 21:18-20) and from entering "the assembly of the Lord" (Deuteronomy 23:1). Philip, who led this eunuch to Christ and baptised him, likely had the eschatological words of Isaiah 56:3-5 in mind. God's Kingdom come had broken human-made barriers of separation. In the words of Paul: "There is neither Jew nor Gentile, neither slave nor free, nor is there male and female, for you are all one in Christ Jesus" (Galatians 3:28). Additionally, these words by Peter would have been freeing to many, including the eunuch: "But you are a chosen people, a royal priesthood, a holy nation, God's special possession, that you may declare the praises of him who called you out of darkness into his wonderful light. Once you were not a people, but now you are the people of God; once you had not received mercy, but now you have received mercy" (1 Peter 2:9-10).

As the church expanded across the Roman Empire, challenges to growth came in the form of physical persecution, spiritual struggles, and doctrinal heresies. The New Testament epistles (Romans through Jude) were written to address these issues. They remind believers that "everyone who wants to live a godly life in Christ Jesus will be persecuted" (2 Timothy 3:12), that our spiritual struggles are not against "flesh and blood," but "against the powers of this dark world and against the spiritual forces of evil in the heavenly realms" (Ephesians 6:12), and that we must "test the spirits to see whether they are from God, because many false prophets have gone out into the world" (1 John 4:1). In the midst of the struggles, they give us hope that nothing can "separate us from the love of God that is in Christ Jesus our Lord" (Romans 8:39), and they challenge us to love others well, which is a command and an invitation that is given over and over to the people of God (Romans 13:9; Gal 5:14; Hebrews 13:1; James 2:8; 1 John 4:21). These epistles reveal that God's desire is not simply to gather people to himself, but, moreover, to help them grow in knowledge, holiness, and mission—to become disciples who disciple others. In other words, the church is both the gathered and the scattered community of Christ in the world.[37]

To summarise, we learned that God gathers others to himself because every person matter to him—his love is all-inclusive and ever-expansive. God's desire has always been that all his creation would come to know and love him. From the beginning, he has been bringing his plan to fruition, drawing the nations to himself. He has been providing a way for them to come to him and in so doing to find true peace and purpose for their own lives. We are called to be like God, a people of inclusivity, acceptance, and love, so that others may experience God's love and be gathered to him and his church, transformed, and sent out to gather others.

The God Who Restores (Revelation)

The main point of the book of Revelation was to bring hope to the church in the midst of trial and persecution and to challenge believers to remain faithful. Revelation is also a reminder to us of God's faithfulness and his continued plan and promise to restore all things; he is indeed the *God who restores*.

We can summarise the book of Revelation in two words—"God Wins!" Likewise, those who have placed their trust in God also win, as does the whole cosmos. Michael Gorman has highlighted five important, sustained, and overlapping narratives in the book of Revelation, which reflect God's purposes and faithfulness. They are worth quoting in whole.

(1) *Creation and re-creation.* This is the story of the faithful, missional, creator God bringing humanity and all creation to its proper end: reconciliation, harmony, and eternal joy in the presence of God.

(2) *Redemption.* This is the closely related story of the faithful, missional, redeemer lamb living, dying, reigning, and coming again to carry out the creator God's mission and create a faithful, missional people.

(3) *Judgement.* This is the story of the faithful, missional God and the Lamb bringing an end to evil as a necessary means for the purpose of re-creation and final redemption.

(4) *Witness: the suffering pilgrim church.* This is the story of a faithful, missional people on earth who have been redeemed by the Lamb and empowered by the Spirit to worship and bear witness to God and the Lamb in spite of danger and persecution.

(5) *Victory: the church triumphant.* This is the story of the faithful, missional people who worship God and the Lamb now and forever in their presence, the appropriate reward for their faithfulness even to death.[38]

These five points provide us with a picture of the consummation of God's master plan, the completion of his grand narrative. They bring together many of the elements of the story that we have highlighted throughout our theological reading of the Bible.

Scripture gives clues to some of the events that will take place as part of this final consummation and restoration. For example, we are told that: Christ will come again (Matthew 24:30; 2 Thessalonians 1:7); the dead will be raised (1 Thessalonians 4:13-18); the elect will be gathered (Matthew 24:31); the world will be judged (Matthew 25:32-46); believers will be glorified (Colossians 3:4); and transformed (1 Corinthians 15:51-52). However, we are clearly told that we will not know the exact time or day when Christ will return (Mark 13:32; Matthew 24:44; Acts 1:7). Therefore, we are called to be prepared at all times (Matthew 25:1-13; 1 Thessalonians 5:6; Revelation 3:2-3, 14-22).

Furthermore, we must remember that when we talk about "the end," it is actually just the beginning. It is a re-creation. Therein, God brings things back to his original intention. Moreover, in God's new creation, God makes his continuous dwelling among the people in a "new earth," and the full impact of the atonement is realised in the termination of sin and death (Revelation 21:1-4; 1 Corinthians 15:54-57). We are also reminded that God has not waited until the end to begin his restoration plan. He has been implementing this plan from the beginning, and God's new creation is already a tangible reality for those who are in Christ (2 Corinthians 5:17). We are God's hands and feet caring for the "least of these" (Matthew 25:34-40); God's voice proclaiming the good news (Romans 10:14-15); and God's love revealing love to others (John 15:9-17). The one, true King God is still on the throne making all things new and he is doing it through the Holy Spirit at work in his church in the world (Revelation 21:5a).

To summarise, we learned that God was, is, and will continue restoring all things because of his covenant faithfulness and his love for his creation; he loves us too much to abandon us and too much to leave us the way we were. God's plan has always been the full restoration of all creation, and this new recreated order will be better than the previous one because God will forever dwell among and in us. We are called to be his people and to reveal the "already and not yet" Kingdom of God to everyone we meet; we join God in his restoration plan by evidencing a new kind of reality in the present.

The Big Picture

Throughout Scripture we see the story of a relational God who creates, calls, provides, accommodates, wrestles, delivers, comes, dwells, gathers, and restore all things in spite of humanity's continued sin, disobedience, and rejection. In this we learn of his deep love for his creation, and thus his desire for humanity to willingly choose to be in relationship with him and to be made holy. We learn about who we are and how we are called to join this relational God in his great redemption plan—not through manipulation, guilt, shame, hate, war, or legalism, but through relationship—by loving him and loving others through God's love!

QUESTIONS FOR REFLECTION

1. In what ways does Christ's incarnation help us understand how we are to love others?

2. How has your understanding of the Kingdom of God changed or grown? Why is a proper understanding of eschatology so important?

3. What stood out to you about the power of the Holy Spirit in the life of the believer? Why?

4. Is the power of the Holy Spirit evident in the witness and unity of your church? If yes, how can you build on this. If no, what steps need to take place to better align with the work of the Spirit?

5. How have you seen God gathering others to himself? How is God calling you and your church to participate in this act of gathering?

6. What about God's restoration plan surprises you, excites you, and worries you? Why?

7. Summarise what you have learned about who God is, what his plan for creation is, and what your role in this plan is? What practical steps can you and your church take in light of these realities?

CHAPTER 5

INTERPRETING THE STORY OF GOD

The word "interpretation" often conjures up images of a translator converting one language into another. However, interpretation is much broader and all-encompassing. Interpretation is the process of trying to bring meaning to an act of communication. It is both necessary and unavoidable, and we do it hundreds if not thousands of times each day. It stands to reason that interpretation is also involved when reading Scripture, which is for the Church a significant means through which God communicates. This reality makes it very important for people, and especially Christians, to have some guidelines to help them to become better interpreters, and from there, better appliers of the Word.

Minding the Gaps

Interpretation is hard enough between two people who know each other, are from the same culture, and speak the same language. However, a change to one or more of these variables and things get exponentially more difficult. This is because these differences are "gaps" in effective communication. When interpreting Scripture, there are multiple real and potential gaps. What follows is just a few of the major gaps of which we should be aware.

Historical and cultural gaps – The people who wrote the Bible and the stories they wrote about took place thousands of years ago. As a result, they were shaped by different places, people, and events than we are. They lived in cultures with unfamiliar norms, values, and laws, and with dissimilar social, political, and religious structures. All these things made them who they were, and they wrote in such a way as to be understood by their original audiences. If we are to understand these words more fully, we must also seek to understand these historical phenomena.

Literary gaps – The books of the Bible are written in a variety of different literary forms (called genres), from the broad categories of narrative, poetry, and letter to more specific genres like wisdom literature, legal codes, prophecy, gospel, and apocalyptic, even sub-genres like call narratives, genealogies, miracle stories, and parables. If the modern reader does not understand how these genres functioned in their historical setting, then he or she will likely misunderstand and misinterpret important aspects of the various books. Readers should also be aware of how certain literary devices function, such as symbolism, metaphor, personification, hyperbole, parallelism, and allusion.

Theological gaps – In a general sense, theology is our understanding about God and how he operates in the world. Different people have differences in theology, some large and others small or even insignificant. This is also the case as we think about the various writers of the Bible and the various communities of which they were a part and to which they were writing. These differences are often tied to their particular experiences, which are tied to their particular historical and cultural contexts. Issues of theology should be considered as part of our reading of Scripture. It is too easy to project our own theological biases upon the text (another word for Scripture as a whole or for a particular passage of Scripture) without giving the authors a voice. If we are not careful, we will shape the Bible more than the Bible shapes us.

Language gaps – The Old Testament was written in Hebrew with a small amount also in Aramaic (about 250 verses out of 23,000). The New Testament was written in Greek. Even for those who know modern Hebrew or Greek or who studied the ancient languages, there are still gaps. This is because language is constantly changing, and the meaning of words are governed by their various contexts. This is especially evident when seeking to understand metaphors, idioms, and slang, which are part of every culture including those represented in Scripture. Even if a person knows the standard dictionary meaning of words, they can be nonsensical outside of their historical contexts.

Translation gaps – Closely tied to language gaps is translation gaps. No translation is perfect, and nuances of meaning are always lost in translation. This is because each language is uniquely tied to its speaker's historical and cultural contexts. Furthermore, we must recognise that a translation is an interpretation of the original communicative act, and the translators are susceptible to the same shortcomings that we face as we interpret Scripture. A good translator tries their best to remove themselves as much as possible from the interpretation. Since the majority of people read a translation of the Bible, it becomes important to understand a bit more about this process and about our modern translations.

Modern Translations

There are four important questions to consider when choosing a modern translation. (1) What theory of translation was used? (2) Which biblical manuscripts did they utilise for their translations? (3) Who were the translators and sponsors of the translation? (4) For what purpose is this translation used?

The three basic theories of translation are *formal equivalence, functional equivalence*, and *free translations*,[39] which function somewhat on a sliding scale. Formal equivalence tries to follow the linguistic form (e.g., vocabulary and grammatical structure) of the original, source language as it comes over into the modern, target language. For this reason, it is often referred to as a word-for-word translation. Functional equivalence, on the other hand, is more concerned with the meaning (or functionality) of the source language as it is translated into the target language. For this reason, it is often referred to as a thought-for-thought translation. Both of these methods have their strengths and weaknesses. Formal translations attempt to keep a level of historical distance and thus cut down on interpretation by following the source text more closely; for this, they are willing to sacrifice some readability. For native speakers of the target language, these translations may feel clunky and be hard to understand. Functional translations attempt to communicate the meaning of the source text to the modern reader in a way that the modern reader can understand. However, such translations usually require more words and a change in word order, which lessens the historical distance and leaves room for the translators to insert more of their own interpretation.

In more recent years, translators and translation committees have often taken a middle ground between formal and functional, producing what can be seen as another category, which is sometimes called *balanced translation*. These translations try to keep the form of the source text whenever possible but are not willing to sacrifice meaning simply to avoid confusion. The final theory of translation, free translation, is a paraphrase of the source material. They are often based off previously translated versions and do not go back to the original languages. In other words, many are translations of translations. Free translations are still concerned with transmitting the meaning of the original texts, but they are equally concerned with the modern reader; some even hope to move the modern reader by the artistic beauty of their prose.

Figure 5 attempts to categorise many of the modern translations. As mentioned above, this is a sliding scale and some of these translations may fit between two of these categories.

Besides the approach behind the translations, it is important to know which biblical manuscripts were utilised for these translations. This is something that few Christians consider, and may be partial due to the complexity of the issue. Many Christians may naively think that the Bible they read was translated from a single source document that had been handed down in its entirety for thousands of years. However, this is not the case at all. We do not possess any of the original books of the Bible, which are known as the autographs. Instead, we possess thousands of copies: fragments of texts, whole texts, whole corpuses (multiple books together), lectionaries, quotations of biblical texts in other works, and early translations in various languages. Unfortunately, with

Formal	Balanced	Functional	Free
King James Version (KJV)	New International Version (NIV)	New Century Version (NCV)	The Living Bible (TLB)
American Standard Version (ASV)	New Revised Standard Version (NRSV)	Contemporary English Version (CEV)	Today's English Version (TEV)
Revised Standard Version (RSV)	Holman Christian Standard Bible (HCSB)	New Living Translation (NLT)	The Message (MSG)
New Jerusalem Bible (NJB)	New English Translation (NET)	Revised English Bible (REB)	The Voice Bible (Voice)
New King James Version (NKJV)	Common English Bible (CEB)	Good News Bible (GNB)	The Passion Translation (TPT)
New American Standard Bible (NASB)			
English Standard Version (ESV)			

(FIGURE 5)

so many copies of copies, there are bound to be differences between the various texts; these are known as variants. Most of these variants are easily explainable as scribal errors, things like omitting a word, repeating a word, and jumbling a few letters that results in a different word.

While this may sound overwhelming, fortunately for the church there was and continues to be a group of amazing men and women who devote themselves to the scholarly discipline known as textual criticism. These people sift through the various manuscripts and other documents to locate and explain the variants and ultimately to produce "critical editions" of both the Hebrew and Greek canons, which take into account all the best copies we possess. The process is reengaged with each new discovery of ancient texts. Indeed, some of the greatest discoveries, which have unearthed some of the oldest copies we possess, have taken place in the past 100 years. Therefore, if a translation of the Bible is based on inferior critical editions, then the reader may be missing out.

This is one of the greatest difficulties with the *King James Version* (KJV) and *New King James Version* (NKJV). The KJV was first translated in 1611 and was based on the best critical texts for that time.[40] Nevertheless, this translation has never been updated based on the hundreds of manuscripts discovered since 1611, many of which are among the earliest manuscripts we now possess. Additionally, when the NKJV was produced in 1982 it was an update of the archaic language of the KJV and did not consult the newer textual evidence that was available. In other words, the NKJV is a reworking of a translation rather than a translation from the original documents.

We do not want to over exaggerate the differences between the KJV/NKJV and other modern translations. Nevertheless, we do not want to ignore these differences either. As an example, there are many additional verses found in the KJV/NKJV, which were attempts to harmonise sections of the New Testament.[41] Most of the newer modern translations either omit these verses altogether or place them in brackets with a footnote informing the reader that these sections are not found in many of the earliest manuscripts (e.g., Mark 16:9-20). Removing them makes little difference doctrinally because they are present in other New Testament books. However, when they are left, they can distort the way we read a particular author's work. Therefore, in the words of Gordon Fee and Douglas Stuart, in their important and best-selling book, *How to Read the Bible for All Its Worth*: "This is why for study *you should use almost any modern translation rather than the KJV or the NKJV.*"[42]

The question of who the translators and sponsors of the translation are can also be important. Many modern versions were translated by a large group of translators chosen from multiple denominations and backgrounds (e.g., NRSV, NIV, CEB, CEV, NASB). This is preferred to a single translator version like *The Message* or *The Living Bible*, which inevitably evidence the translator's own experiences, culture, and theology. Additionally, sometimes knowing the sponsoring body behind a translation tells us a lot about its possible theological and cultural biases. For example: the *American Standard Version* was sponsored by British scholars from multiple denominations; the *New Jerusalem Bible* was sponsored by the Roman Catholic Church; and the *Holman Christian Standard Bible* was sponsored by LifeWay Christian Resources of the Southern Baptist Convention.

The final question for choosing a modern translation is more personal. For what purpose is this translation being used? If your main concern is for personal devotional reading or if you are wanting to recommend a version to a new believer, then you may want to choose a version from the functional or free list. However, if your main concern is in depth study, whether personal or in preparation to lead a group or preach a sermon, then you should choose and compare a few versions from both the formal and balanced list.

Interpreting the Bible

There are two important technical words used to speak about the process of biblical interpretation. The first is exegesis, which is derived from a Greek word meaning "to lead out." Traditionally, the process of exegesis is seen as a primarily historical investigation that seeks to discover the intention of the author—what the author was trying to communicate to his[43] original readers. "It has to do both with what he said (the content itself) and why he said it at any given point (the literary context)."[44] This is often contrasted with eisegesis, meaning "to lead in." This is when we read into the text what we want it to say, rather than seeking to understand what the text was saying.

The second term is hermeneutics, which is derived from a Greek word meaning "interpretation." Exegesis and hermeneutics are often used interchangeably. Nevertheless, hermeneutics has a broader meaning that encompasses both the act of biblical interpretation (exegesis) as well as the philosophical questions of understanding and meaning and the anthropological and sociological questions about the interpreter and his or her worldview.[45] In other words, hermeneutics is not just concerned with the historic text, but also with the modern reader. When we think about the full scope of biblical interpretation, we must consider what has often been termed *the three worlds of the text*, which includes: *the world behind the text, the world of the text,* and *the world in front of the text.*

The world behind the text is centred on the author and the events surrounding the writing of the text. It seeks to understand the historic author who wrote the book, his historic community and its cultural and social norms, and the historic events that took place in and around the author and his community. It is also concerned with understanding the traditions that sit behind certain words, ideas, and actions, the earlier oral forms of various stories, and the source documents that a particular author or editor utilised. This world seeks to address the historical and cultural gaps mentioned above.

The world of the text is centred on the text and is especially concerned with addressing the literary gaps mentioned above. This world recognises that while Scripture is sacred, it is still literature and as such operates by many of the same rules as other types of literature. Therefore, it can be evaluated using many of the same tools and methods. For this reason, it seeks to understand the genre and sub-genres found in each biblical book and to understand how they function to express meaning. It looks at structural elements like plot, setting, and characterisation as well as style, tone, point of view, syntax, and diction to understand the overarching purpose and flow of the literature. It examines the use of literary and rhetorical devices and looks at how various authors quote and allude to other biblical writings.

The world in front of the text is centred on the modern reader and on theology. This would be the most controversial of the three worlds. Some scholars would argue that there is no place for inserting the modern reader into the interpretive process. Nevertheless, others would argue that it is impossible to avoid such an insertion. By acknowledging the role of the modern reader, we are able to do several things: to name and claim the biases and presuppositions of the modern reader, which helps to lessen these phenomena in the interpretive process; to evaluate the text from new angles based on the starting place of the various modern readers (e.g., gender, culture, experiences), which has the possibility of challenging the way we have traditionally read a particular passage; and to contextualise the application to meet the needs of the modern reader and his or her community. This world also evaluates how the passage and the modern reader's interpretation fits into the grand narrative and theology of the whole of Scripture and seeks to hear what others, especially the early church, said about any given text.

When these three worlds of the text are utilised in our interpretation of Scripture, our interpretations have the potential to bridge the various gaps, to move us toward more accurate understanding of the particular texts under evaluation and of the Bible as a whole, and to help us form a more holistic theology and a more contextual application, all of which equals greater impact in the life of the believer and in the life of the church.

For some, this type of critical evaluation seems a bit sacrilegious. Are we really called to put Scripture under such a microscope? And where is the work of the Holy Spirit in our reading of Scripture? These are important questions. Hopefully, the Holy Spirit is at the centre of our study and interpretation of the Bible. We as the church, both individually and corporately, are filled with the Holy Spirit and as such, we should invite the Holy Spirit into this process regularly and consistently.

Nevertheless, we are also aware that many godly women and men have had very differing interpretations of Scripture, and many ungodly men and women have distorted Scripture to gain power and to manipulate others. God gave us brains and the ability to reason for a reason. One of these reasons is so that we can dig deeply into the Scriptures seeking to understand truth, and so we can discuss, even rigorously debate (in love), with each other Scripture's meaning and how to apply it in any and every circumstance and context. Each of us brings our own experiences to the table of interpretation and application, and this is a good thing. However, our ability to reason, both individually and corporately, as well as the traditions (historic interpretations and orthodox theology) of the church are a safeguard to bad interpretation and application.

A Brief Guide for Interpreting Scripture

The first rule of biblical interpretation is that "the text has a voice." This means that we must learn to listen and to hear. In the case of a written document such as Scripture, this also means that we need to learn the art of careful and analytical observation. This section is designed to help each person to hone his or her skills of observation and biblical interpretation in a way that takes into account the three worlds of the text as well as experience, reason, and tradition. This "guide" is broken into four sections with multiple questions that help the modern reader to observe the text more closely and to ask critical questions of it (the full guide[46] is found in Appendix 1).

Instead of just reading through this guide and the comments, it may be beneficial for you to pick a passage of Scripture and work through this exercise. As you do, there will likely be questions for which you do not have the answers. That is okay! Many of these answers are readily available in study Bibles, Bible dictionaries, introductory biblical textbooks, and in Bible commentaries. Also, do not be alarmed if you do not own these types of secondary sources, many are available online. Nevertheless, a word of warning—not every source you find online is helpful or credible (see Appendix 2 for a list of trusted online websites). If you are planning on doing a lot of biblical interpretation, then it is probably worth investing in a few good background resources. As we begin, it is worth re-emphasising that the initial task is focused on reading, observing, and listening to the biblical text. The secondary resources just mentioned should only be engaged as noted in the guide, which is especially near the end of the process.

Section 1 – Preliminary Work

a. Begin by selecting a passage of Scripture to interpret.

If this is your first time, it is good to start with a shorter passage of Scripture, between 5 and 10 verses (do not pluck a single verse or two out of context). Most modern translations split texts into subtitled sections, which can be helpful for selecting a coherent passage. However, you should recognise that the title of these sections is not part of the original Hebrew and Greek texts. In other words, they are part of the translators' interpretation. Try not to let these titles dictate or guide your interpretation.

b. Take time to pray and ask the Holy Spirit to guide you as you read and interpret this passage.

Remember, interpreting Scripture is a spiritual act that should not be done in your own strength or wisdom. Pray for God to focus your mind and heart and for him to help you listen and see anew. Also pray that God will help you to find concrete ways to apply that which you are studying.

c. Read through the biblical book multiple time seeking to understand the main themes and the flow of the book.

Sometimes, we mistakenly think that we only need to read the passage of Scripture that we have selected for study. This is not enough, and such an approach can quickly and easily lead to misinterpretation. The various books of the Bible were written or edited together as a whole, and as such, they tell a larger story together that is meant to guide the reader toward certain understandings and actions. For this reason, you need to comprehend the main themes and the flow of the book as a whole. Obviously, some biblical books are quite long and reading through them multiple times will take a significant amount of your time. Nevertheless, this is not a race. The goal is greater understanding of the Bible as a whole and greater growth in your faith. As you read through, take notes that include key words and ideas you are seeing. Do not forget to read the book in a few of the different modern translations that we talked about above.

d. Make a list of any presuppositions you have about your passage or about the book as a whole.

This includes ideas you have heard from others through sermons, books, etc. Often without knowing it, we allow previous interpretations of a text to guide the way we read or hear it the next time. This is especially true if the interpretation came from someone you respect, a favourite author or pastor. This is not to say that their interpretations were wrong. However, it is a good practice to set aside such biases or presuppositions so that you listen anew to what God might be trying to teach you. Additionally, after you have done your interpretation, you may have some of these presuppositions confirmed and others refuted.

Section 2 – The World Behind the Text: Historically Grounded Questions

a. Who is the author and what do we know about him?

Knowing who the author of a particular book is can be very helpful. It provides important information that may give you a fuller picture. For example, if you know that the writer of the Gospel of Matthew is believed to be Matthew the tax collector turned disciples of Jesus, then you already have insight into his background and his experiences. If you do not know the answer to this question, you may want to do a bit of research now or set it aside for later in the process. In your research, you may find that the authorship of some books is contested or unknown (e.g., Deuteronomy, Hebrews). Not being able to identify the author does not cripple your interpretation.

b. Who is the audience and what do we know about them?

Similarly, knowing who the audience is can help you do additional research that will strengthen your understanding and your interpretation. For example, if researching 2 Corinthians, knowing the history, geography, social norms, and religious diversity of Corinth would be very helpful, as would knowing the issues and struggles this community has already faced as noted in 1 Corinthians. Remember to take good notes that can be used again later. If saving your research till later in the process, then be sure to write out the questions you wish to research later.

c. When was this book written and what is important about this period for the author and audience?

We are all shaped by events that have taken place in history, especially those that we personally experienced. Knowing a bit of the history surrounding the timeframe of a particular book can help you empathise with what the audience might have gone though. For example, Revelation was written during a time when Rome was persecuting Christians. This information helps explain some of the struggles and the use of covert, symbolic language. You will need to do some research for this question. Be careful not to let this research distract you from your primary purpose of better understanding and interpreting your text. As you read, you may find other interesting things you want to research later. Write them down and come back to them when you have more time.

d. What is the overarching purpose of this book?

Having read the book containing your passage multiple times and possibly having done some light historical research, now is the time for you to sum up the overarching purpose of the book in your own words. In essence, you are seeking to articulate the answer to the question: "What is the author trying to accomplish through this book?" As an example, you may deduce that the purpose of Isaiah is: "To warn Israel about the consequences of sin and to reveal God's plan for redemption and restoration of all the nations." As you construct this statement, think about your particular passage and how it fits into and extends this purpose. This statement does not need to be perfect, you can refine it as you move forward.

e. Are there any other historical, cultural, or religious issues that need to be investigated further to help you understand the context of the author, audience, your passage, or the book as a whole?

This question can be especially fruitful if you are willing to read for what you do not already know and to acknowledge the possibility that some concepts, events, and situations that may appear familiar to you may have different meanings in their historic context. For example, as you read Psalm 23, you might explore the concept of "shepherd" in the Old Testament and discover its connection to kingship. Or you may explore the custom of a host anointing a person's head with oil and learn its cultural and religious significance. The more questions you are willing to ask and explore the greater possibility for deeper interaction with the historic context of your passage and the greater possibility for more accurate interpretation.

Section 3 – The World Within the Text: Literary Grounded Questions

a. What is the literary genre of the book and of the particular passage under investigation?

The genre, or literary type, helps the reader understand how to approach and analyse a book and passage. If you are unsure, consult secondary sources. There is a link to a "Genre Guide" by Roger Hahn and Dennis Bratcher in Appendix 2, which will help you understand the basics of how to interpret the various genres.[47] For example, if the biblical book under investigation is Proverbs, you will want to understand the genre of wisdom literature and the difference between speculative and proverbial wisdom.

b. Looking at the book as a whole, what are the major and minor themes?

As you read through your biblical book, you will notice multiple themes running throughout, some minor and others major. Consider how these themes help fulfil the purpose you listed above (step 2d). As you look at these themes, you may want to refine your purpose statement. Also consider which of these themes is most important for the passage you are evaluating. For example, some of the major themes of Isaiah are God's holiness, justice, and righteousness, the impending consequences for dis-obedience, the Servant of Yahweh, and God's redemption and restoration of the nations. If you are exegeting Isaiah 49, then the Servant of Yahweh theme is significant, and you can ask how this Servant helps to fulfil the larger purpose in the whole of the book.

c. Looking at the immediate context, the passages that come directly before and after your passage, do these passages help you understand your passage better?

It is very important to evaluate the immediate context of your passage. Often your passage will be part of a larger argument, a larger section, or a particular theme in the book. Carefully consider the connections between these passages and the journey they are trying to take the reader on. Some passages can take on radically different meanings than you may have thought when they are read in their literary contexts. A perfect illustration is the often-quoted words of Jeremiah 29:11—"'For I know the plans I have for you,' declares the Lord, 'plans to prosper you and not to harm you, plans to give you hope and a future.'" This verse sits within a passage telling Judah to make themselves comfortable in the land of exile because they would be there for some time and it was not God's desire to deliver them at this point. Furthermore, the passages that precede and follow this chapter give two examples of false prophets giving the people erroneous information and misguided hope about deliverance. In its context, Jeremiah 29:11 is still a passage of hope and trust but moreover, it is a passage about patience and the long journey toward humble repentance.

d. Are there repeated words, phrases, or ideas in your passage, the immediate context, or the whole book? How are they connected?

This is where looking at multiple modern translations and utilising a formal version can be helpful. Many translations will translate the same Hebrew or Greek word differently based on the immediate context in which it is found. Therefore, you may miss the repetition of some words. A prime example is Paul's multiple and differing use of the Greek word *sarx* (translated as "flesh," "body," "human being," and "sinful nature"). When finding multiple repeated words, phrases, or ideas, consider how they are connected and how they might differ from each other. Furthermore, if the author has written more than one book of the Bible, then you may want to see if he utilises any of these same words or ideas in his other writings. Remember to always bring it back to your passage and ask how these findings shed light on your text and help you better interpret what is trying to be communicated.

e. Are there any biblical texts that are cited or clearly alluded to in your passage? What is the context of the cited text? Are there connecting words, themes, theological ideas? Can you determine why this text is being cited?

The biblical authors often quote or allude to earlier sections of Scripture. Usually, this is a case of a New Testament author pointing back to a passage of Scripture from the Old Testament. However, it can also take place within the same testament. The good news is that you do not need to have the whole Bible memorised in order to catch these quotations and allusions. Most modern Bibles contain a scriptural index that indicates quotations and allusions and where the source text may be located. It is important to recognise such references and to understand the connection being made by the author as it can significantly increase your understanding and sharpen your interpretation of the passage. The most common reasons for an author to quote or allude to an earlier passage of Scripture is to (1) draw the reader into the previous story, (2) to give support to the current argument, or (3) to provide an analogy. An example of the latter is seen in Paul's use of the Abrahamic story in Galatians 3 and 4.

f. As you take all the above information into account, what are the key ideas in your passage?

If you are studying a longer passage, consider dividing the text into an outline with sections. Give a short title to each section that encompasses the main idea of that section. This is your first attempt to summarise and order what you have learned from careful evaluation of your passage in its context. Breaking down and outlining your passage can provide significant insight into your understanding of what and how the author is trying to communicate. In essence, it gives you a visual look at your interpretation. Notice, this is not just a general outline of your text; it is meant to be an interpretive outline. The difference can be seen in the example from Ruth 1:6-18 (see figure 6).

General Outline	Interpretive Outline
1:6-18 – Naomi and her daughters-in-law	1:6-18 – The faithful love of God in human form
1:6-10 – Naomi's first plea; Orpah's and Ruth's refusal	1:6-10 – Naomi's plea for God to show faithful love toward her daughters-in-law
1:11-14 – Naomi's second plea; Orpah's acceptance, Ruth's refusal	1:11-14 – Naomi's misunderstanding concerning God's faithful love toward her
1:15-18 – Naomi's third plea; Ruth's adamant refusal; Naomi's concession	1:15-18 – Ruth as an example of God's continued faithful love toward Naomi

(FIGURE 6)

Do not be discouraged if you struggle with this task. Such an interpretive outline takes practise. As an alternative, you might consider writing an interpretive paraphrase of the passage that attempts to capture the same thing that the interpretive outline is meant to capture.

g. How do these key ideas fit into the larger purpose the author is trying to fulfil in this book? Is it consistent? If not, is there another way of interpreting this passage?

This step is an important safeguard in the interpretive process. You should be able to see a connection between the key ideas and purpose you have stated for your passage (step 3f) and the overall purpose you stated for the book (step 2d). If a connection cannot be made, then you should consider re-evaluating your interpretation of the particular passage, the book as a whole, or both.

h. Create a "summary statement" that attempts to capture the main idea of the passage in your own words.

This statement should be clear, simple, and emphasis your understanding of the key idea or ideas. An example from Psalm 23 might be: "David writes this song of thanksgiving to highlight his absolute trust in God, even in the midst of difficult times."

Section 4 – The World in Front of the Text: Theologically Grounded Questions

a. How does your interpretation of this passage fit into the larger theological narrative of Scripture? Is it consistent? If not, is there another way of interpreting this passage?

The first three steps in this section are additional safeguards, but on a larger scale than step 3g. The current step requires that you have a good understanding of the grand narrative of Scripture and the theological doctrines that are both found within and constructed through careful, systematic analysis of the whole (Hopefully, chapters three and four will have given you a starting place for answering this question). It is important to understand how the individual passage you are interpreting fits into the larger whole, both narratively and theologically. This process deepens and strengthens your theological understandings and tests its consistency and cohesion. At points, you will be challenged to reinterpret your current text or to re-evaluate your current larger theological construct in light of what you are learning from the smaller parts. This is a healthy process that shows spiritual and intellectual maturity.

b. How does your interpretation of this passage fit into your own theological worldview? Is it consistent? If not, is there another way of interpreting this passage? Or, if not, do you need to re-examine any of your theological positions?

This step is a slightly narrowed version of the previous one as it looks specifically at your own theological worldview. For most people reading this book, this will be a Wesleyan perspective. If you are unsure of the main tenants of your particular denomination or church, be sure to do some study in this area. For Wesleyans, a good starting place is the book *Exploring a Wesleyan Theology* by David McEwan, which is part of this series (Frameworks for Lay Leadership).[48]

c. What have others said about this passage? Is there anything that they have said that makes you need to re-examine your passage in light of this new information?

This is one of the places where more in depth study of secondary literature is both appropriate and important. If you set aside research from the earlier step until later, now is the time for it. Additionally, consulting commentaries, which are books focused on the interpretation of Scripture, is a way of assuring that you have not completely misrepresented the meaning of your passage or have not missed something substantial in your interpretation. It is important that this step takes place at this point and time rather than earlier in the interpretative process so that someone else's interpretation of the passage does not become a lens for your own reading. While it is true that the writers of these commentaries are usually well-trained scholars, this does not mean that they have the only "correct" interpretation of Scripture. Furthermore, many commentaries have little or no application, and those that do cannot possibly know your situation and context and, therefore, cannot give you appropriate, concrete application. If the goal is greater personal understanding and application, then you must be committed to the whole process and prayerfully attentive to the Holy Spirit.

d. What are the theological implications of your interpretation of this passage?

Both this step and the next are arguably the most significant. Nevertheless, they are really only possible (and most fruitful) when they come at the end of this process of listening and interpreting. This step will also provide you with the information to more accurately answer the questions in steps 4a and 4b, to which you may want to return after you have addressed this question. Here, you are trying to address the same three questions we explored in chapters 3 and 4: (1) What do we learn about the character of God?; (2) What do we learn about God's plans for all creation?; (3) What do we learn about our role in the unfolding story? The only difference is that you are considering your specific passage as you address these questions.

***e. What are the practical applications of your interpretation of
this passage? What are some steps that can be taken to live out
this truth in your context?***

This is the big "so what" question. It is the opportunity to find tangible
and concrete ways to apply the truth of the passage in your context. You
must be careful not to make the application too general. Saying that the
passage is calling you to pray more or help those in needs may be true,
but you would do better to be more specific and to find ways that the
text is trying to strengthen your faith by stretching you out of your com-
fort zone. Good application often begins with honest self-assessment. For
example, understanding where you are in your faith journey, what your
temptations and weakness are, and what is currently shaping your worth
and identity, will provide you with more personalised application that
will most likely have greater impact in your spiritual growth. Similarly, if
you are seeking to apply the interpretation of your passage to a community through teaching, preaching, or outreach, you will need to understand the community and assess its needs in order to better contextualise
your application.

The Hermeneutical Spiral

Hopefully the above process was helpful in guiding us toward more
faithful interpretation and more fruitful application. Some readers may
have noticed a circular or spiralled pattern within the process as we
transitioned from big picture to small picture and back again multiple
times. We moved from our pre-understanding, to exegesis of a particular passage in its larger contexts, to locating the specific interpretation
into a larger theological construct, to applying this information within
one's life and ministry. In light of this progression, we are then invited to
return to our starting place and revaluate our pre-understanding. In this
way, there is a continual movement and refinement of our understanding, interpreting, and applying of God's word; this is the hermeneutical
spiral.

QUESTIONS FOR REFLECTION

1. Which of the five "gaps" in effective communication do you struggle most with in understanding Scripture? How can you improve your understanding in this area?

2. What are some things that surprised you about modern translations of the Bible? How has this information helped you?

3. How do you understand the modern interpreter and the Holy Spirit to work together in the process of hermeneutics?

4. Were there any steps in the *Brief Guide for Interpreting Scripture* that you struggled with? Why do you think you struggled with these particular steps?

5. What steps in the *Guide* do you think are most helpful and why?

6. If you worked through the *Guide* with your own passage, how do you feel about the interpretive conclusions and applications you reached? Are you willing to share these with your Christian community to evaluate, challenge, and confirm your readings of Scripture?

7. Why is the hermeneutical spiral important in the interpretive process?

8. What are the benefits for yourself, for your local church, for the greater church, and for the world, of Christians taking the full process of biblical interpretation more seriously?

CHAPTER 6

CONTINUING
THE STORY OF GOD

The reality of a living Word is that it moves forward, speaking into the lives of people in each new generation as they engage the text. Like Jacob and the people of Israel, who find identity in their struggle with God, we are invited to wrestle with the Word[49] and in so doing to find deeper intimacy with God and reliance upon him. This idea is beautifully captured in the words of David Jasper speaking about how the Jews approached their Scriptures: "The Jews did not so much seek meaning in words, but rather saw in words a form of conversation, which is endless and reaches no conclusion, unless it is finally enclosed into the silence of God with which everything begins and ends."[50]

As already noted, Scripture is more than a dead book where we go to find information. The Bible is a meeting place where we discover who God is and who we are in God. Therein, we have an ongoing invitation to embrace the living Word, to be transformed in our thinking, being, and doing. In so doing, we give God the final word in our lives.

A Hermeneutic of Love

As we considered the grand narrative of Scripture in chapters 3 and 4, God's love was evident from start to finish. This truth is significant! If love is fundamental to who God is and what he does (1 John 4:9-10, 16), and if love is central to who we are as Christians (Matthew 22:37-39), then we should seriously consider how this love informs our interpretation of the Bible, both in its parts and as a whole. It is therefore viable to speak about a hermeneutic of love, where love is defined by God and not based on human sentimentality or an "anything goes" mentality. A few other modern scholars have proposed love as a lens for our reading of Scripture.[51] Nevertheless, this concept can be traced back to Augustine around 400 AD. He said: "Whoever, then, thinks that he [or she] understands the Holy Scriptures, or any part of them, but puts such an interpretation upon them as does not tend to build up this twofold love of God and our neighbour, does not yet understand them as he [or she] ought."[52]

Augustine understood that our interpretations must remain true to what we know about God through the whole of Scripture. This point has already been highlighted in the interpretation guide in chapter 5 (steps 4a, b, d). As noted, our larger theological reading of Scripture serves as a safeguard for our interpretation of any particular passage. Some people may consider a hermeneutic of love to be naïve or disingenuous, especially in light of the exegetical focus of seeking to discover the authorial intention. Augustine had an answer for this as well. He wrote: "If, on the other hand, a man [or woman] draws a meaning from [the Scriptures] that may be used for the building up of love, even though he [or she] does not happen upon the precise meaning which the author whom he [or she] reads intended to express in that place ... he [or she] is wholly clear from the charge of deception."[53] In other words, we are always called to err on the side of love.

If we hold to a dynamic theory of inspiration, we recognise the possibility that some passages in the Bible may reflect the human authors' theologies and worldviews, rather than reflecting a full picture of God. Additionally, we can be assured that our own human interpretations are often flawed; as we engage difficult passages from different angles, we may discover interpretations that align with both the author's intention and the overarching grand narrative. John Wesley had a similar approach when he combatted an erroneous theology of predestination, which tried to limit God's selection to an elect few; a view that he believed denied God's love and was not actually supported by Scripture. He wrote: "No Scripture can mean that God is not love, or that his mercy is not over all his works."[54] As Christians, especially those coming from a Wesleyan perspective, we have a responsibility to find ways to understand and explain difficult passages of Scripture that appear to present a contradictory picture of God. This "may also require us to elevate certain aspects of the Bible that appear to be the more dominant and overarching themes, such as love, grace, peace, [justice] and human value, as well as the overarching narrative of God's restoration through human participation."[55]

Above all, we must remember that we are the *imago Dei* in our world. Our words, actions, and even our interpretations of Scripture, project a picture of God to our world. The question we must constantly ask ourselves, both personally and corporately, is: "Are we representing God accurately?"

Conclusion

Hopefully this small book has instilled a level of confidence within each of us, encouraging us to engage the Bible more fully. We are reminded of the words of 1 John 4:18—"There is no fear in love. But perfect love drives out fear, because fear has to do with punishment. The one who fears is not made perfect in love." We should not be afraid to delve deeply into God's Word to understand him more and, in so doing, to understand ourselves better. If our motive is genuine relationship, then we are able to approach God and the Bible with a reverent boldness. We can be assured of God's love for each one of us, and we can be confident that he will meet us where we are and challenge us to be more like him. We can be assured that God desires to transform us and use us to carry out the *missio Dei* in the world. We are the Church, and we have been called to continue the story of God in the places where God places us.

QUESTIONS FOR REFLECTION

1. What do you see as the advantages and disadvantages of a hermeneutic of love?

2. How would you apply a hermeneutic of love to Deuteronomy 20:10-18 and 1 Samuel 15:1-3? To what other passages or issues would you apply this hermeneutic?

3. In what tangible ways can you continue the story of God in your local context?

SUGGESTIONS FOR FURTHER STUDY

Beginner

Fee, Gordon D. and Douglas Stuart. *How to Read the Bible for All Its Worth*. Third edition. Grand Rapids: Zondervan, 2003.

Hamilton, Adam. *Making Sense of the Bible: Rediscovering the Power of Scripture Today*. New York: HarperOne, 2014.

McKnight, Scot. *The Blue Parakeet: Rethinking How You Read the Bible*. Grand Rapids: Zondervan, 2008.

Schenck, Kenneth. *Making Sense of God's Word*. Indianapolis: Wesleyan Publishing House, 2009.

Thompson, David L. *Bible Study that Works*. Anderson, IN: Francis Asbury, 1994.

Intermediate to Advanced

Bartholomew, Craig G. and Michael W. Goheen, *The Drama of Scripture: Finding Our Place in the Biblical Story*, second edition (London: SPCK, 2014).

Callen, Barry L. and Richard P. Thompson, eds. *Reading the Bible in Wesleyan Ways: Some Constructive Proposals*. Kansas City: Beacon Hill Press, 2004.

Green, Joel B. *Reading Scripture as Wesleyans*. Nashville: Abingdon,

2010.

Lodahl, Michael. *The Story of God: A Narrative Theology*. Second edition. Kansas City: Beacon Hill Press, 2008.

Varughese, Alex, et al., eds. *Discovering the Bible: Story and Faith of the Biblical Communities*. Kansas City: Beacon Hill, 2006.

Wall, Robert W. and David R. Nienhuis, eds. *A Compact Guide to the Whole Bible: Learning to Read Scripture's Story*. Grand Rapids: Baker Academic, 2015.

Wright, N. T. *Scripture and the Authority of God: How to Read the Bible Today*. New York: HarperOne, 2011.

A BRIEF GUIDE FOR INTERPRETING SCRIPTURE

1. Preliminary Work

    a. Begin by selecting a passage of scripture to interpret.

    b. Take time to pray and ask the Holy Spirit to guide you as you read and interpret this passage.

    c. Read through the biblical book multiple time seeking to understand the main themes and the flow of the book.

    d. Make a list of any presuppositions you have about your passage or about the book as a whole (This includes ideas you have heard from others through sermons, books, etc. Try to set these aside for the time being as they can often control/alter your interpretation.)

2. The World Behind the Text: Historically Grounded Questions

    a. Who is the author and what do we know about him?

    b. Who is the audience and what do we know about them?

    c. When was this book written and what is important about this period for the author and audience?

    d. What is the overarching purpose of this book? (What is the author trying to accomplish through this book?)

    e. Are there any other historical, cultural, or religious issues that need to be investigated further to help you understand the context of the author, audience, your passage, or the book as a whole?

3. The World Within the Text: Literary Grounded Questions

    a. What is the literary genre of the book and of the particular passage under investigation? (e.g. narrative, poetry, law, gospel, etc.)

    b. Looking at the book as a whole, what are the major and minor themes? (This is usually the strategy for fulfilling the purpose)

    c. Looking at the immediate context, the passages that come directly before and after your passage, do these passages help you understand your passage better?

    d. Are there repeated words, phrases, or ideas in your passage, the immediate context, or the whole book? How are they connected?

    e. Are there any biblical texts that are cited or clearly alluded to in your passage? (These can often be found in your Bible's footnotes). What is the context of the cited text? Are there connecting words, themes, theological ideas? Can you determine why this text is being cited? (It is often used to [1] draw the reader into the previous story, [2] give support to the current argument, [3] provide an analogy).

    f. As you take all the above information into account, what are the key ideas in your passage? (If a longer passage, consider dividing the text into an interpretive outline with sections. Give a short title to each section that encompasses the main idea of that section. You may also consider making an interpretive paraphrase of the passage.)

g. How do these key ideas fit into the larger purpose the author is trying to fulfil in this book? Is it consistent? If not, is there another way of interpreting this passage?

h. Create a "summary statement" that attempts to capture the main idea of the passage in your own words.

4. The World in Front of the Text: Theologically Grounded Questions

a. How does your interpretation of this passage fit into the larger theological narrative of Scripture? Is it consistent? If not, is there another way of interpreting this passage?

b. How does your interpretation of this passage fit into your own theological worldview? Is it consistent? If not, is there another way of interpreting this passage? Or, if not, do you need to re-examine any of your theological positions?

c. What have others said about this passage? Is there anything that they have said that makes you need to re-examine your passage in light of this new information?

d. What are the theological implications of your interpretation of this passage? (What does it teach you about God, God's plan, humanity's role?)

e. What are the practical applications of your interpretation of this passage? What are some steps that can be taken to live out this truth in your context?

TRUSTED ONLINE WEBSITES

Biblical Studies Resources

- Ancient Near Eastern Sacred Texts: *www.sacred-texts.com/ane*

- Best Commentaries: *www.bestcommentaries.com*

- Bible Gateway: *www.biblegateway.com*

- Bible Study Tools: *www.biblestudytools.com*

- Biblical Studies: *www.biblicalstudies.org.uk/index.html*

- Blue Letter Bible: *www.blueletterbible.org*

- Catholic Resources: *catholic-resources.org/Bible/Exegesis.htm*

- Christian Classics Ethereal Library: *www.ccel.org*

- Early Christian Writings: *www.earlychristianwritings.com*

- Early Jewish Writings: *www.earlyjewishwritings.com*

- Genre Guide: *www.whdl.org/sites/default/files/media/Bangkok2017-Fringer-Handout%20-%20Genre%20Criticism.pdf*

- NT Gateway: *www.ntgateway.com*

- N. T. Wright Page: *ntwrightpage.com*

- OT Gateway: *www.otgateway.com/pentateuch.htm*
- OT Story: *otstory.wordpress.com/web-resources-for-ot-studies*
- Paul and Scripture: *paulandscripture.blogspot.com*
- The Paul Page: *www.thepaulpage.com*

Wesleyan Based Resources

- A Plain Account Lectionary: *www.aplainaccount.org*
- Australasian Centre for Wesleyan Research: *acwr.edu.au*
- Christian Resource Institute: *www.crivoice.org/index.html*
- Didache: *didache.nazarene.org*
- Methodist and Wesleyan Studies Collection: *www.globethics.net/ web/gtl/collections/methodist-and-wesleyan-studies-collection*
- NTS Center for Pastoral Leadership: *cpl.nts.edu/index.php/ resources*
- Seedbed: *www.seedbed.com*
- The Discipleship Place: *discipleshipplace.org*
- Wesleyan Holiness Digital Library: *whdl.org*
- Wesley Center Online: *wesley.nnu.edu*

NOTES

1 James Barr, *The Semantics of Biblical Language* (London: SCM Press, 1983), esp. 206-65. Note also the importance of Semantic range in determining meaning.

2 N. T. Wright, "How Can the Bible be Authoritative? (The Laing Lecture for 1989)," *Vox Evangelica* 21 (1991): 9.

3 Cf. N. T. Wright, *Scripture and the Authority of God: How to Read the Bible Today* (New York: HarperOne, 2011), 20. Wright says, "the phase 'authority of scripture' can make Christian sense only if it is a shorthand for 'the authority of the triune God, exercised somehow *through* scripture,'" emphasis his.

4 Daniel Castelo and Robert W. Wall, "Reading the Bible as Scripture," in *A Compact Guide to the Whole Bible: Learning to Read Scripture's Story*, edited by Robert W. Wall and David R. Nienhuis (Grand Rapids: Baker Academic, 2015), 25.

5 Paul Enns, *The Moody Handbook of Theology*, revised and expanded (Chicago: Moody, 2008), 158-59.

6 H. Orton Wiley, *Christian Theology*, Volume 1 (Kansas City: Beacon Hill, 1940), 176.

7 Roger E. Olsen, "Is the Bible 'Inerrant' or 'Infallible'?," found at *http://www.patheos.com/blogs/rogereolson/2015/11/is-the-bible-inerrant-or-infallible* (accessed 20 March 2018).

8 *Church of the Nazarene, Manual 2017–2021: History, Constitution, Government, Sacraments and Rituals* (Kansas City: Nazarene Publishing House, 2017), 27. This statement closely aligns with the statement of the United Methodist Church, which closely aligns with the statement of the Anglican Church, from which John Wesley came.

9 See Michael Lodahl, *All Things Necessary to Our Salvation: The Hermeneutical and Theological Implications of the Article on the Holy*

Scriptures in the Manual of the Church of the Nazarene (San Diego: Point Loma, 2004), 29-31.

10 The numbers in this chart indicate the standard order in which these 24 books are found in the Hebrew Bible. Sometimes these are divided differently with Judges-Ruth and Jeremiah-Lamentations combined giving a total of only 22 books.

11 Dating of the biblical books varies considerably. For example, some maintain a much later starting date ranging from 1200 – 750 BC, and some maintain an earlier ending date of around 400 BC.

12 Cf. Michael J. Broyde, "Defilement of the Hands, Canonization of the Bible, and the Special Status of Esther, Ecclesiastes, and Song of Songs," *Judaism* 44.1 (1995): 65-79. Some other books may have been considered authoritative by early Jewish Rabbis and especially the Hebrew version of Wisdom of Ben Sira. See Michael Satlow, "The Wisdom of Ben Sira: How Jewish?," found at: *https://thetorah. com/the-wisdom-of-ben-sira-how-jewish* (accessed 18 January 2018).

13 Roger T. Beckwith, *The Old Testament Canon of the New Testament Church: and its Background in Early Judaism* (Eugene, OR: Wipf & Stock, 2008), 76-77.

14 We should also note the significance of the Dead Sea Scrolls, which were discovered in a series of caves near Qumran in the 1940's and 50's. Of the more than 800 manuscripts discovered there, about 220 were copies of Old Testament books, which included all but Esther and Nehemiah.

15 Craig L. Blomberg, *Can We Still Believe the Bible? An Evangelical Engagement with Contemporary Questions* (Grand Rapids: Brazos, 2014), 47-51. Nevertheless, there does appear to be allusions to these books in the New Testament.

16 James H. Charlesworth, "The Wesleys and the Canon: An Unperceived Openness," *Proceedings of the Charles Wesley Society* 3 (1996): 63-88.

17 This quotation has been modernised. It is attributed to Jerome in various places including the Anglican Communions "Thirty-nine Articles of Religion," found at: *http://www.anglicancommunion. org/media/109014/Thirty-Nine-Articles-of-Religion.pdf* (accessed 4 February 2018).

18 Blomberg, *Can We Still Believe the Bible*, 55-56.

19 Lee M. McDonald, "Lists and Catalogues of New Testament

Collections," in *The Canon Debate*, ed. Lee M. McDonald and James A. Sanders (Peabody, MA: Hendrickson, 2002), 591-98.

20 Wright, *Scripture and the Authority of God*, 116.

21 For a fuller picture of this loving, relational God see: Rob A. Fringer and Jeff K. Lane, *Theology of Luck: Fate, Chaos, and Faith* (Kansas City: Beacon Hill, 2015).

22 Paul R. Williamson, *Sealed with an Oath: Covenant in God's Unfolding Purpose* (Downers Grove: InterVarsity, 2007), 44.

23 Gordon J. Wenham, *Exploring the Old Testament, Volume 1: A Guide to the Pentateuch* (Downers Grove: InterVarsity, 2003), 86.

24 John Goldingay, *Old Testament Theology Volume 1: Israel's Gospel* (Downers Grove: IVP Academic, 2003), 534-538.

25 Cf. Goldingay, *Israel's Gospel*, 544-548.

26 Carol Meyers, "Temple, Jerusalem," *The Anchor Bible Dictionary Volume 6 Si-Z*, edited by David N. Freedman (New York: Doubleday, 1992): 350-369

27 See Fringer and Lane, *Theology of Luck*, 69-72.

28 Dennis Bratcher, "Patterns for Life: Structure, Genre, and Theology in Psalms," found at: *http://www.crivoice.org/psalmgenre.html#Lament* (accessed 11 January 2018).

29 Alex Varughese, et al., eds., *Discovering the Bible: Story and Faith of the Biblical Communities* (Kansas City: Beacon Hill, 2006), 185.

30 Gordon D. Fee and Douglas Stuart, *How to Read the Bible for All Its Worth*, Third Edition (Grand Rapids: Zondervan, 2003), 187.

31 T. F. Torrance, *Incarnation: The Person and Life of Christ*, ed. Robert T. Walker (Downers Grove: InterVarsity, 2008), 95, 106.

32 Ajith Fernando, *Acts*, The NIV Application Commentary (Grand Rapids: Zondervan, 1998), 90-91.

33 Cf. Richard S. Briggs and Joel N. Lohr, eds., *A Theological Introduction to the Pentateuch: Interpreting the Torah as Christian Scripture* (Grand Rapids: Baker Academic, 2012), 47-49.

34 Dean Flemming, *Recovering the Full Mission of God: A Biblical Perspective on Being, Doing and Telling* (Downers Grove: IVP Academic, 2013), 135.

35 G. R. Beasley-Murray, *Gospel of Life: Theology in the Fourth Gospel* (Peabody, MA: Hendrickson, 1991), 82.

36 Scot McKnight, *1 Peter*, The NIV Application Commentary (Grand Rapids: Zondervan, 1996), 23-24.

37 For more information on this subject see: Hugh Halter and Matt Smay, *And: The Gathered and Scattered Church* (Grand Rapids: Zondervan, 2010).

38 Michael J. Gorman, *Reading Revelation Responsibly: Uncivil Worship and Witness: Following the Lam into the New Creation* (Eugene, OR: Cascade Books, 2011), 38.

39 For more information on this subject see: Fee and Stuart, *How to Read the Bible*, 33-55; and Michael J. Gorman, *Elements of Biblical Exegesis: A Basic Guide for Students and Ministers*, Revised and Expanded Edition (Grand Rapids: Baker Academic, 2009), 35-59.

40 *Masoretic Text* for Hebrew and *Textus Receptus* for Greek

41 See Lincoln H. Blumell, "A Text-Critical Comparison of the King James New Testament with Certain Modern Translations," *Studies in the Bible and Antiquity* 3 (2011): 67-126, for a list of the 21 most significant differences.

42 Fee and Stuart, *How to Read the Bible*, 40, emphasis theirs.

43 The masculine pronoun is used because it is believed that all the biblical authors were male. Although, some have argued a female for the writing of the book of Hebrews.

44 Gordan D. Fee, *New Testament Exegesis: A Handbook for Students and Pastors*, Third Edition (Louisville: Westminster John Knox, 2002), 1.

45 For more on Hermeneutics see: Anthony C. Thiselton, *Hermeneutics: An Introduction* (Grand Rapids: Eerdmans, 2009).

46 This "guide" is a significantly modified and simplified version of the one found in Jeannine K. Brown, *Scripture as Communication: Introducing Biblical Hermeneutics* (Grand Rapids: Baker Academic, 2007), 275-80.

47 Additionally, see Fee and Staurt, *How to Read the Bible for All Its Worth*.

48 David B. McEwan, *Exploring a Wesleyan Theology*. Frameworks for Lay Leadership, edited by Rob A. Fringer (Lenexa, KS: Global Nazarene Publications, 2017).

49 Geoffrey Hartman, *The Third Pillar: Essays in Judaic Studies* (Philadelphia: University of Pennsylvania Press, 2011), 17-31.

50 David Jasper, *A Short Introduction to Hermeneutics* (Louisville: Westminster John Knox, 2004), 25-26.

51 E.g., N. T. Wright, *The New Testament and the People of God* (Minneapolis: Fortress, 1992), 64; Alan Jacobs, *A Theology of Reading: The Hermeneutics of Love* (New York: Routledge, 2002).

52 Augustine, *On Christian Doctrine*, I.36.40, found at: *http://www.ccel.org/ccel/augustine/doctrine.xxxvi.html* (accessed on 26 January 2018).

53 Augustine, *On Christian Doctrine*, I.36.40, found at: *http://www.ccel.org/ccel/augustine/doctrine.xxxvi.html* (accessed on 26 January 2018).

54 John Wesley, "Sermon 110: Free Grace," *The Works of John Wesley: Volume 3, Sermons III 71-114*, ed. by Albert C. Outler (Nashville: Abingdon, 1986), 556.

55 Fringer and Lane, *Theology of Luck*, 178.

FRAMEWORKS FOR LAY LEADERSHIP

ABOUT THE EDITOR

Rob A. Fringer, PhD–Principal and lecturer in Biblical Studies and Biblical Language at Nazarene Theological College in Brisbane. Rob is an ordained elder in the Church of the Nazarene and has 15 years of pastoral experience working in the areas of Youth, Adult Discipleship, and Community Outreach. He is co-author of *Theology of Luck: Fate, Chaos, & Faith* and *The Samaritan Project* both published by Beacon Hill Press of Kansas City. Rob is married (Vanessa) and has two children (Sierra and Brenden).

BOOKS IN THE
FRAMEWORKS FOR LAY LEADERSHIP SERIES

ENGAGING THE STORY OF GOD
Rob A. Fringer

EXPLORING A WESLEYAN THEOLOGY
David B. McEwan

EMBODYING A THEOLOGY OF MINISTRY AND LEADERSHIP
Bruce G. Allder

ENTERING THE MISSION OF GOD
Richard Giesken

EXPRESSING A NAZARENE IDENTITY
Floyd Cunningham

EMBRACING A DOCTRINE OF HOLINESS
David B. McEwan and Rob A. Fringer

www.ingramcontent.com/pod-product-compliance
Lightning Source LLC
Chambersburg PA
CBHW021137020426
42331CB00005B/809

*9 7 8 1 5 6 3 4 4 8 9 1 1 *